MICRO-BUDGET *Hollywood*

Budgeting (and Making) Feature Films for $50,000 to $500,000

BY PHILIP GAINES AND DAVID J. RHODES

SILMAN-JAMES PRESS
Los Angeles

First Edition
10 9 8 7 6 5 4 3 2 1

Library of Congress Cataloging-in-Publication Data

Gaines, Philip.
Micro-budget Hollywood : budgeting (and making) feature films for
$50,000 to $5000.000 / by Philip Gaines and David Rhodes
p.   cm.
Includes filmographies.
1. Motion pictures—Production and direction. 2. Low budget motion
pictures. 3. Motion picture industry—United States—Finance.
I. Rhodes, David J.   II. Title.
PN1995.9.P7G342   1995   791.43'023—dc20   95-12009

ISBN: 1-879505-22-3

Cover design by Heidi Frieder

Printed and bound in the United States of America

SILMAN-JAMES PRESS
distributed by
Samuel French Trade
7623 Sunset Blvd.
Hollywood, CA 90046

MICRO-BUDGET Hollywood

Contents

Acknowledgments

First of all, of course, we are grateful to all out interviewees, whose names need not be repeated here, for their candor. For helping us contact other people, additional thanks are due to Chuck Cirino, Peter Jensen and Alain Silver, and Nicole Libresco. In this regard, we also need to thank Bob Hoover, Fred Lombardi at *Daily Variety,* and Siobhan McDevitt at Concorde for trying to hook us up with the king, whom we hope is feeling better.

Shardell Cavaliere at Cast and Crew Payroll kindly provided the most up-to-date fringe percentages. Mark Ean assisted with the sample pages printing. Ron Dawson at Movie Magic got us a review copy of his company's budgeting program and arranged for permission to reproduce it (with the attendant free publicity).

Once again we must thank our editors at Silman-James, Jim Fox and Gwen Feldman, for making us count every word, and Jim Fox for making us weigh them, too. Now if they'd only sell some more copies of these books, we could retire to some exotic location.

The underlying form of the sample budget is reprinted by permission and, we are asked to notify you, is: Copyright © Sceenplay Systems, Inc. Movie Magic™ and Screenplay Systems™ are trademarks of Screenplay Systems, Incorporated.

Preface

We're back. We hope that all of you who read *Hollywood on $5,000, $10,000, or $25,000 a Day* were able to put that information to good use. We got a lot of positive feedback on that book and only one or two death threats.

Since the publication of our previous opus, many of our readers and colleagues in the industry have asked for a detailed sample budget, a line-by-line guide on how to spend what money they have. As we explained in the first book, budgets in the abstract have only so much usefulness. What you may reasonably expect using the leverage you have on one project to the max may get you nothing on another. Nonetheless, the first part of this book is a sample budget and an account-by-account, line-by-line explanation of how to use it.

Perhaps we should pause briefly and define terms. We threw the expression "micro-budget" around a lot in *Hollywood on $5,000* without ever pinning down exactly what we meant. People have laid claim to making feature films for ridiculously low amounts. We extolled Robert Rodriguez in the last book for his remarkable *El Mariachi* and its $7,000 budget. But, as if participating in a parsimonious variant of "Name that Tune," where the cry is "I can make that movie for just X dollars," micro-budgeteers have reached new lows. There is a gentleman offering a one-day class through a local learning emporium who claims to have shot a video feature (and transferred it to film) for a mere $2,000! One of our interview subjects cites the same figure. We'll let the appropriate book of world records sort all that out. Let's be realistic here. Yes, you or anyone can make a movie for under $100,000. We have, and it's not an experience we would ever wish to repeat. Many people are making healthy profits producing kickboxing extravaganzas for a quarter of a million dollars and selling them in bulk to the foreign buyers who annually descend on Santa Monica for the AFM. (That's the American Film Market, not the American Federation of Musicians.) So we've decided to let the market dictate the cost of a micro-budget show and set the high-end total at $500,000.

Make no mistake about this: $500,000, $250,000, $125,000—none of these are chump change. No matter what your movie-funding treasure map says, you will not find that amount of money under a rock. And we are certainly not suggesting that you talk your gray-haired Aunt Sadie into letting you take a flier with her nest egg. Moviemaking at any level is not only risky business, but it's full of slicksters ready to steal your goods. For those who want to self-finance (or use a portion of Aunt Sadie's nest egg), we will present some "micro-plus" alternatives. But we're never going to tell you how to make a video feature for six dollars and a case of soda pop. If you cannot come up with at least $15,000 or preferably $30,000, then put this book back on the shelf until you have filled those 2,000 quart jars with pennies.

For those doubting Thomases out there, in part two of this book you will meet, via transcribed interviews, a gaggle of actual micro-budgeteers. Some of these people are legends of the low-budget world, who grind out these micro-epics year in and year out and seldom fail to turn a profit. Others are, like us, one-timers who used that first micro-budget effort as a springboard to bigger and better (what other alternative could there be?) pictures.

We are not endorsing or even suggesting that you spend your money on one of the software budgeting programs that are available commercially. They may be more than you need to spend for a micro-budget show. Nor are we telling you to buy and/or to refer to any other of the books already published and available on budgeting. They are mostly keyed to normal, i.e., multi-million-dollar, budgets, and none of them will offer you concepts tailored to the micro-budget. But this is just the first utterance of a disclaimer that we hope will not be repeated *ad nauseam* (yup, we still like using Latin): This is not a book about basic budgeting. It would be more apt to say that it's a book about minimalist budgeting (forgive us for resorting to such trendy terminology, but apt is apt). It is not necessarily about minimalist filmmaking. That is up to you.

Part One

THE MICRO-BUDGET

Yes, here are still more introductory remarks. They are pertinent, so please read them carefully.

There are many budget formats in use. Each studio has its own chart of accounts, as do many independents. Most of them conform to the type reproduced here in the way they organize those accounts. The simple fact is, for micro-budgeting purposes, most of these accounts don't matter. Actually, none of the "account numbers" means anything. They are, by definition, an arbitrary designation. If you are going to be doing cost reports on your picture, then those account designations (the four-digit numbers) will (or should) be used by whomever does the accounting to add up the costs by category. And if you are going to use account numbers, you might as well use some that approximate what the rest of the production world uses.

Enterprise Printers in Hollywood has long produced two basic forms: (1) a short form in which the below-the-line production accounts are broken into two broad categories: personnel and equipment; and (2) a long form, almost exactly like the one reproduced here, which uses the studio method of assigning each production department its own account that includes both personnel and equipment. In the short form, all the crew (or "Production Operating Staff") are in Account 9 and the equipment is in Account 11 ("Set Operations"). Thus the Sound Mixer is in Account 9 and his or her Nagra would be in 11. On the long form, "Set Operations" is used to designate Grips, Labor, Painters, and the like and includes both people and materials.

Confused? In the "studio method," where each department is, theoretically at least, responsible for administering its own budget, the choice is clear. Each department should be a separate account and all of that department's costs are broken down within. Ironically, in the micro-budget world, this format also has much to recommend it and for exactly the same reason. If the art department has all of $200 with which to buy what it needs, then it makes sense for that $200 not to be lumped in with the money for the grip's dulling spray, the makeup person's sponges, or the costumer's dress shield's (those little pads that are sewn into the underarms to prevent sweat stains, which it's a good idea to put in the producer's shirts, also).

Of course, if there is no formal "art department," if one person is taking care of props, set dressing, clothes, and bringing the snacks, too, then it might make sense to resort to a simpler format. That doesn't mean the short form. It, too, will have much more detail than the bring-your-own-equipment, super-ultra-micro-budget show will need. The best alternative is to extract the needed "line items" onto a shorter form. In the long-form sample that follows, even with the cast detail and personnel salaries broken down into prep/shoot/wrap, there are less than 200 line items, that is, lines of detail in the budget, with actual dollar amounts attached. Obviously, this could easily be condensed into four or five pages of detail.

Why use the long form? Two reasons: First, while micro-budgeteers have a narrower range of possibilities, the particular line items may vary considerably from project to project. You may not need an animal handler, a water wagon, or travel insurance but another show will. Having them already in place in whatever master form you start with not only saves typing, it reminds you of which items are needed as you read through it. Second, and this is a little less direct in concept, the empty lines are very important because they tell you what you don't have money for. What that means is that you would like to have a still photographer, but you can't afford to pay one. So you budget for film and processing and get a friend with a Nikon to come by on occasion. You may well want to annotate this in your budget as an allowance of zero dollars, a salary of no money per week for three weeks, or a payment that is zeroed out by an offsetting deferment. Or you can just write in the budget, "My pal Tony will come by and take pictures two or three times a week for free." If there is no still photographer in your budget form, you may have to tie a string around your finger to remember, and on most pictures, you'll need more than ten little reminders (or twenty if you wear sandals without socks) such as this.

The long form reproduced here—we just happened to have a recent budget for an actual (unmade) picture in our computer—was created using the Movie Magic program and their "ENTERPRZ" form. We are not endorsing Movie Magic over the several other companies that sell budgeting and breakdown programs for both PC and Mac; but Movie Magic does seem to be the most commonly used. All these programs will produce a straightforward budget and, if you use their "global" templates, permit rapid comparisons of alternative schedules, locations, etc. The only complaint we have about Movie Magic is that it wouldn't accommodate our picture title, *Desire Under the Magnolias*, in the header, hence the abbreviation. None of these programs are cheap, either. You can buy a couple hundred of the printed blank forms from Enterprise for the cost of one of these programs. Obviously, using a calculator and adding fringe percentages by hand takes more time than entering these numbers into a specialized computer program. But if you are dealing with less than 200 line items, it still should not take more than a day of concentrated work.

This takes us back to square one. Obviously, any budget is meant to reflect the estimated cost of producing an item—from a bird house to a hotel. Most movies fall somewhere in between those two, but again the fundamentals are simple. For all of the above,

you need two manners of things. You need materiel and you need experienced people to manipulate that materiel. What any budget estimates is the cost of acquiring that materiel and hiring those people. Before you budget, you must answer two questions: how much and how many? How much does that cost, and how many of them do we need? Most of these questions will be "answered" by the script (and again we refer you to the precepts we offered in *Hollywood on $5,000, $10,000, or $25,000 a Day*). How many actors is easy—you just count them. How many days is more complicated, but still is a factor of the contents of the script. Actors are in particular scenes, which will require a specific number of days to shoot. Remember that in the micro-budget world, even on SAG productions, actors need not be paid for "hold" days. Total shooting days will always be a compromise between the "ideal" dictated by the script and the "real" dictated by the amount of money you have.

Okay, here come the rudimentary examples. As you will see, most of the quantitative answers are simply the products (we're talking in the mathematical sense here, i.e., the result of multiplying two or more numbers) of various factors. First, "how much"? How much film, for instance. Well, all formats run at so many frames per second and have so many frames per foot. You manipulate that to get a final footage. Ninety minutes of 35mm is calculated in the following equation:

90 minutes x 60 seconds x 24 frames = 129,600 frames ÷ 16 (frames per foot) = 8,100 feet

We've taken you the long way around from merely giving the standard "90 feet per minute" to make the point about factoring. On a micro-budget, you can factor or you can rely on budgeting "rules of thumb." There are two "rules of thumb" about film, which we will *not* be using. Rule No 1: normal budgets would use 10,000 feet as the final length. Micro-budgeteers cannot afford that extra 1,900 feet. But there are some heads and tails to the reels and you may want to add a minute or two over 90, so 8,500 feet is our proposed micro-budget substitute rule of thumb. Again, remember that the script answereth all. If it's short, cut this figure down. If it's long, cut the script down or add film. Obviously, in 35mm you will actually shoot considerably more than 8,100 or 10,000 feet of film. Here, the normal rule of thumb (No. 2) is 5,000 feet per day. What's the micro-budget answer? Factor from the final length, first, and shooting days, second. Normal budgets expect a ratio of between 10:1 and 30:1, that is, 100,000 to 300,000 feet of film for a 10,000-foot final picture. Micro-budgets should fall between 2:1 and 6:1. Again, remember the script. Are there special circumstances? A film with just a few characters talking will have a lower ratio (i.e., fewer feet of film used) than a picture with action scenes or many characters.

Does this seem a bit complex for a rudimentary example? It's not. The mathematics are simple. The complication is in picking the factors, and that's what the budgeting process is all about. You have read the script, and you know how much money you have. When you budget, you will select from the range of factors that conform to your knowledge, and you will enter those factors into the formulas already on the budget form to produce dollar totals. The only information that you must acquire from somewhere other than the script are the fixed, unit costs.

Film, as it happens, is sold, processed, and printed by the foot. And, if you've read our first book, you already know that not only do all those prices vary from vendor to vendor, but they are also negotiable. Normal budgets do not count on special deals or discounts. Micro-budgets need them to survive. You don't need to have a signed contract or even a preliminary discussion with a vendor to estimate a cost. You can even plan on getting something for free (remember your pal Tony, the still man).

Besides free, there are two types of entries for any line: (1) how much/how many and (2) allowances. How much and how many are best expressed as factors: X people at X amount per week for X number of weeks. The budget forms will accommodate the two or three factors necessary. Allowances are expressed as a flat fee or amount of dollars. Some may refer to services that you can estimate at this stage of the budgeting process, such as an allowance for parking on location. Until you find locations and know what the parking requirements are and what facilities are available, you have no alternative but an allowance. Other allowances are conventional. For example, you will be copying scripts and other documents, which will run into thousands of pages. But it is not really necessary to guess at a total number of copies and multiply that by so many cents per page. In instances like this you will follow common practice and simply "allow" a total amount.

If, at this point, you still don't believe us about the lack of mystery in budgeting, you have two alternatives. One, you can go out and buy one of those "normal" budgeting books. They'll have plenty of anecdotes and more information about Greensmen and Mounting Charges (no, that's not what you pay stunt people whenever they climb on their horses) than any mirco-budgeteer would ever need. Or two, you can read on. Look at the lines in the budget and the comments on the facing pages. If you see a term that you don't understand in those comments, check out the glossary in *Hollywood on $5,000, $10,000, or $25,000 a Day*. If it's a term on an empty line of the budget itself, don't just forget about it—your show might still need some of whatever it may be.

A final note on the budget form. You will notice six columns in each account: "Amount," "Units," "X," "Rate," "Subtotal," and "Total." The Movie Magic template permits up to three factors ("Amount," "X," and "Rate") and allows lines of detail within each account. Don't use these unnecessarily. In many instances, you will only have two factors, such as 45,000 ("Amount") feet ("Units") of film at 37 cents ("Rate") per foot. There are shorthand keys for the common units (Days, Weeks, Hours, etc.), so these don't have to be typed in each time. If there is nothing in the "X" column, the program will assume a "1" when it performs the multiplication. In most cases, you will only use the lines of detail if the rates vary. Under Production Staff, Account 2000, for example, all the variables are used. You will notice here that there are different rates for shooting weeks, and some persons have a fraction of a week for prep. The times should refer to the "Units" and not the "Rate." In the Production Staff examples, "0.60" and "0.20" are used to indicate 3 days or 6/10 of a five-day week and 1 day respectively. If you prefer, you can enter "3 (Amount) Days (Units)," leave the "X" column blank, and change the Rate to 1/5 of the weekly amount. Both methods are in common use.

Acct #	Description	Page #			Total
1100	Story & Other Rights	1			3,000
1200	Producer	1			2,500
1300	Director	3			5,000
1400	Cast	4			33,059
1500	Travel & Living	5			0
1600	Miscellaneous	5			500
1900	Fringe Benefits	5			9,013
	TOTAL ABOVE-THE-LINE				53,072
2000	Production Staff	6			15,980
2100	Extra Talent	7			14,850
2200	Art Direction	8			3,600
2300	Set Construction	9			0
2400	Set Striking	9			0
2500	Set Operations	10			9,170
2600	Special Effects	11			0
2700	Set Dressing	12			7,255
2800	Property	13			4,700
2900	Men's Wardrobe	15			4,350
3000	Women's Wardrobe	15			1,020
3100	Makeup & Hairdressing	16			4,020
3200	Elec., Rigging & Oper.	17			11,540
3300	Camera Operations	18			15,220
3400	Sound Operations	19			7,350
3500	Transportation	20			24,110
3600	Location	21			33,800
3700	Prod. Film & Laboratory	22			30,525
3800	Stage Facilities	23			0
3900	Process & Rear Projection	23			0
4000	2nd Unit	24			0
4100	Tests	25			250
4900	Fringe Benefits	25			17,124
	TOTAL PRODUCTION PERIOD				204,864
5000	Editing	26			12,400
5100	Music	27			7,500
5200	Post Production Sound	28			18,300
5300	Post Prod. Film & Lab.	29			14,360
5400	Main & End Titles	29			5,000
5900	Fringe Benefits	30			2,221
	TOTAL EDITING PERIOD	30			59,781
6500	Publicity	30			750
6700	Insurance	30			16,250
6800	General Overhead	31			3,500
7500	Fees, Charges, & Misc.	31			3,500
7900	Fringe Benefits	31			62
	TOTAL OTHER CHARGES				24,062
	TOTAL ABOVE-THE-LINE				53,072
	TOTAL BELOW-THE-LINE				288,707
	ABOVE & BELOW-THE-LINE				341,779
	Contingency 5 %				17,089
	Overhead 0 %				0
	Completion Bond 0 %				0
	GRAND TOTAL				358,868

The Top Sheet

The Top Sheet summarizes the total budget. The totals of each individual section or each account are entered here. Most Top Sheets also have a "Header" with information such as the title of the project, shooting days, start and end dates, and the like. Depending on the form and/or program you are using, you can fill those in as you like, but they are not really pertinent to this discussion

All Top Sheets also divide the budget into two broad areas: Above-the-Line and Below-the-Line. The concept is simple. Above the line is talent: writer, producer, director, and actors. Below it is technical crew and equipment. Extras swing both ways, depending on the form, but are mostly below, despite what SAG would have you believe. Most budgets separate below into production, post-production, and a catch-all of overhead items from insurance to offices.

In normal budgets, there is more of a balance between the lines. In our sample budget, the underlying assumption is that the major creative talents in writing, producing, and directing will earn very little, and the actors will work for "scale," or Screen Actors Guild minimums. Of course, there are other ways to go. We once saw a $100,000 budget (exclusive of post costs) in which the Writer/Producer/Director took a fee of $12,000. The reasoning was that there would be nothing without him and he needed something for six months of his time. Other micro-budgets may include a disproportionately large sum for a single actor.

If it takes some unusual allocation to make the project, then make the allocation or forego the project. Micro-budgets are not about appearances, or about what's normal or usual. They're about what makes it happen and what works for the money.

Acct #	Description	Amount	Units	X	Rate	Subtotal	Total
1100	**Story & Other Rights**						
1101	Story Purchase						0
1111	Screenplay Purchase						
	Writer Fee	3,000	Allow		1	3,000	3,000
1114	Sequel Rights						0
1121	Secretary						0
1131	Copying						0
1141	Research and Clearance						0
1151	Script Timing						
							0
1161	Script Consultant						
							0
						Total for 1100	3,000

Story & Other Rights

The script should cost little or nothing. As we so cunningly remarked in our last book, if all the scripts in Southern California were suddenly thrown into the Pacific, the high tide would send waves lapping against the Hollywood sign. Seriously, on a micro-budget project, you can expect to get a writer on your project who will work for the experience (and credit, of course) only. Do pay at least one dollar to make it a work-for-hire so that you can retain copyright.

There also are professional writers who specialize in micro-budget scripts, and they do expect to be paid a flat fee for their work. The amount we have budgeted is an allowance for this kind of writer. They may also want deferments, points, etc.; but that's a wordsmith of another color. This discussion is confined to cash.

"Research and Clearance" refers to the kind of script report that must be generated to satisfy certain Errors and Omissions policies (see Account 6700). You really should avoid any script, for instance, based on real people or events of the immediate past. Private people, or those not publicly known, retain the rights to their own lives. But even public people have rights to the portion of their lives that is not common knowledge *and* cannot be slandered by a fictional depiction. We're not lawyers, so if you must make this kind of picture on a micro-budget (bad idea though it may be), get some legal advice.

Acct #	Description	Amount	Units	X	Rate	Subtotal	Total
1200	**Producer**						
1201	Producer(s)						
	Living Allowance	250	WEEKS		10	2,500	2,500
1211	Executive Producer(s)						
							0
1221	Co-Producer(s)						
							0
1231	Production Executive(s)						
							0
1251	Secretary(ies)						
							0
1271	Assistant(s)						
							0
1285	Other Charges						
							0
					Total for 1200		2,500

Producer

The producer or producers may often go uncompensated in micro-budgets, on the assumption that he, she, or they will reap their rewards from the profits. Of course, the rent et al. continue to be due, so it is not unreasonable to include what we have labeled a "Living Allowance."

It would be nice to afford Secretaries, Assistants, and the like. Later, you may be able to. In the meantime, perhaps you can convince some young, eager film-school graduate to do it for the chance to learn, get a credit, work on the next, bigger-budget project–you know, all those valuable intangibles.

We're not going to try to explain what a producer does, but at this budget level all you need is one intelligent, honest person watching the store. If that's not you, it can be a Producer, Line Producer, Production Manager, whatever you want to call that person who will ultimately administer this budget. You don't need more than one, and unless there is a compelling reason (for example, the Production Manager is getting a Producer credit so the Production Coordinator would like the Production Manager credit, none of which costs anything . . . you get the idea), you should not have more than one person in charge of controlling costs. It's just more food to buy. If you are controlling costs and doing something else as well (such as directing or starring), then get someone to *assist* you in producing. Give them a lovely credit and a few bucks. Like we said in our last tome, someone who doesn't have a clue (i.e., no experience) in micro-budget is worse than no one at all. Turn your back on someone like this for a couple of moments and he or she may have made enough bad deals out of ignorance to totally blow your budget.

Acct #	Description	Amount	Units	X	Rate	Subtotal	Total
1300	**Director**						
1301	Director(s)	5,000	Allow		1	5,000	5,000
1305	Second Unit Director(s)						
							0
1306	Dialogue Directors						
							0
1307	Secretaries						
							0
1311	Casting Director						
							0
1315	Casting Assistant(s)						
							0
1341	Location Casting						
							0
1351	Personal Assistant(s)						
							0
1385	Other Charges						
							0
					Total for 1300		5,000

Director

If you, the person who bought this book, are not the director, then we assume that whoever the director may be, that person has a reason, other than a large, up-front fee, for wanting to direct a micro-budget enterprise. Perhaps you don't have a director yet and would like to hire James Cameron. If so, it's time to go to your second choice. Then third, then fourth, and so on, until you come up with someone who will work for around $5,000.

If the director is essentially a partner in the project and a major participant in the profits, then the only reason to pay any money is the same one that indicated a "living allowance" for the producer. If you are hiring a director and not offering a piece of the profit pie, then you will likely end up with a person who has need of a feature credit, however micro it might be. If that person has experience in music videos, industrials, or in some capacity on features, you will obviously be offering him or her an opportunity that will have a value beyond cash.

In a perfect world, it would also be good to have a casting person, assistants, etc. In the micro-budget world, you will have to do most of these stray above-the-line chores yourself (and probably a few below-the-line chores, too, before you're through).

As with the writer, the fee to the director is a cash allowance and does not include fringes. More on that below.

Acct #	Description	Amount	Units	X	Rate	Subtotal	Total
1400	**Cast**						
1401	Stars						
	MANDY	3	WEEKS		1,647.80	4,943	
	ANGIE	3	WEEKS		1,647.80	4,943	
	FRED	3	WEEKS		1,647.80	4,943	
	MR. CUTTER	1.40	WEEKS		1,647.80	2,307	
	DAVIS	1	WEEK		3,500	3,500	20,636
1421	Supporting Cast						0
1441	Day Players						
	TAMMY	3	DAYS		475	1,425	
	JEFF	3	DAYS		475	1,425	
	CAROL	2	DAYS		475	950	
	JUDGE	1	DAY		475	475	
	MR. ANTHONY	1	DAY		475	475	
	ELLIS	1	DAY		475	475	5,225
1471	Stunt Coordinator	1	WEEK		1,607	1,607	1,607
1473	Stunt Personnel	6	DAYS		431	2,586	2,586
1475	Stunt Adjustments						0
1481	Overtime						
	Allowance	30,054	%	0.10	1	3,005	3,005
1483	Looping, Fitting, etc.						0
1485	Other Charges						0
	Additional Cost Re: Cast						0
					Total for 1400		33,059

Cast

Those of you who carefully read our first book will remember how much we respect and admire the members of the Screen Actors Guild. Notice in the cast account, however, how large a sum is required even for the few actors that our hypothetical micro-script requires. Don't forget that SAG now represents extras as well, an issue which we will revisit in Account 2100.

What to do? Shouldn't the micro-budgeteer go non-SAG if at all possible? What prevents you from going non-SAG? Well, perhaps a SAG member is putting up the money and directing this picture. It's been known to happen. Or perhaps you have raised your limited financing based on the commitment of a particular SAG actor to a specific part. Whatever the reason, if you must become a SAG signatory, you must pay everyone, not just the SAG members, no less than scale.

The numbers here are the SAG "low budget" minimums effective through July 1, 1995. They are not much lower than normal scale, as the real break in the SAG low-budget deal is that you need not pay Day Players for "hold" days, that is, work days between when they begin and end their services on which you are shooting scenes with others. SAG Actors also get paid Fringes, both Union and, unless they have a loan-out corporation, Governmental. There's more detail in the Fringe account, which follows shortly. But the bottom line is that this adds about 30% to your cost. This particular budget automatically breaks out Fringes into separate accounts at the end of each budget sub-division. If you are using a printed form and making entries by hand, don't forget to add in Fringes.

Non-SAG actors may be hired on a non-salaried, non-fringed, "fee" basis. Before you decide to do this, see the further discussion under Account 1900, Fringes.

Even under the low-budget agreement, SAG actors get overtime. The only break is that the overtime rate remains at time-and-a-half for up to 12 hours of total work time. 10% represents an average of less than one hour per day. The daily rate is for 8 hours, so here's the formula: 1 hour at time-and-a-half equals one and a half times 1/8th of the daily rate or 3/16ths or 18.75% or

$$1.5 \times .125 = .1875 = 18.75\%$$

That means a 10% allowance buys you all of 32 minutes. The weekly overtime rate is even more cumbersome; but the bottom line is, on a 15-day shoot, 10% is hardly realisti; it's just all you can afford. There are ways around this problem, and there are details in *Hollywood on $5,000, $10,000, or $25,000 a Day* about how to circumvent scale, but that doesn't help in the budgeting phase.

Travel & Living

Travel & Living are expenses that you should try to avoid. SAG has rules about what constitutes a Distant Location. In fact, you can travel outside the studio zone—that thirty-mile circle drawn around the Beverly Connection (if you really want to know why it's centered there, check the first book)—if your cast agrees not to tell. But why go that far unless some extremely compelling location demands your presence?

Miscellaneous

$500 should cover a multitude of sins in the Miscellaneous category. This is not the type of show where you'll be buying gift baskets to put in the cast's motorhomes on the first day of shooting.

Acct #	Description	Amount	Units	X	Rate	Subtotal	Total
1500	**Travel & Living**						
							0
1501	Travel & Living Expenses						0
1511	Accommodations						0
1521	Per Diem						0
1551	General Allowance						0
3385	Other Expense						0
						Total for 1500	0
1600	**Miscellaneous**						
1600	Miscellaneous		Allow		500	500	500
						Total for 1600	500
1900	**Fringe Benefits**						
1901	Payroll Service Charges						
	SAG payroll	25	Chks		8	200	200
1999	Fringes						
	FICA	6.20	%		33,059	2,050	
	SUI/FUI	6.20	%		19,423	1,204	
	Medicare	1.45	%		33,059	479	
	Workers' Comp.	2.73	%		30,054	820	
	SAG - Actor	12.85	%		33,059	4,248	
	Payroll Charges	0.25	%		4,612	12	8,813
						Total for 1900	9,013

Fringe Benefits

Fringe Benefits are those troublesome little add-ons imposed by the governments and unions. The basic complement of fringes are broken down on the budget page: FICA (Social Security), SUI/FUI (state and federal unemployment insurance), and Medicare (self-explanatory). You can, if you prefer, lump these together. However, because the cut-offs, or the maximum amount on earnings on which the fringe is imposed in any tax year, vary, computerized micro-budgeteers may want to save every penny and take advantage of the program's ability to set each one. You can buy Workmen's Compensation coverage from an insurance broker, directly from the state fund in California, or through a payroll service, which is the simplest and usually the cheapest way to go. Because they are insurances, SUI/FUI and Workmen's Comp rates will vary from company to company, based on their history of claims, so shop around. The rates here (from Cast and Crew Payroll) are about as low as one can expect.

The only persons fringed in the above-the-line portion of the budget are the Actors. Some payroll services will charge by the check ($8 to $12) on Actors and other above-the-line personnel. On normal shows, this is usually cheaper than .25% ($4 per $1,000), but not here. As we said in our first book, a payroll service is a great bargain. They make all required fringe payments, they are the employers of record for unemployment-claim purposes, and they do the W-2 and 1099-MISC tax reporting at the end of the year. Unless you've got a strong accounting background, don't get involved in doing this yourself.

As we mentioned above, we are assuming that other major creative persons will be paid a fee. Technically, unless the Producer and the Director have personal-service corporations to loan out their services, payment of a fee is not the proper way to do it. But "independent contractors" are quite common in the film industry. In fact, everyone on your micro-budget, non-union cast and crew can be paid on this basis.

The key issue is who can be considered a vendor of a service, that is, someone who contracts to provide a service for a fee, and who must be considered an employee. Persons who report to a site that you specify or are required to be present during a work day that you define or merely work under the supervision of someone else could all be considered employees. We discussed the legal implications of treating an employee as a contractor with regard to payroll taxes and workmen's compensation in *Hollywood on $5,000, $10,000, or $25,000 a Day*. In a nutshell, you are at risk in many areas when you engage a person as an "independent contractor" who actually meets the definition of an employee. Not too many people on a crew meet such basic criteria as setting his or her own hours and schedule or working without supervision. Audits can leave you liable for both portions (employer *and* employee) of the Social Security (FICA) payments, IRS penalties for not withholding, and, in California, problems with the Labor Board over hourly pay and overtime. There are some alternatives, which we'll discuss in Account 4900.

Acct #	Description	Amount	Units	X	Rate	Subtotal	Total
2000	**Production Staff**						
2001	Production Manager						
	PREP	2	WEEKS		450	900	
	SHOOT	3	WEEKS		600	1,800	
	WRAP	1	WEEK		450	450	3,150
2005	Unit Production Manager						0
2011	First Assistant Directors						
	PREP	2	WEEKS		400	800	
	SHOOT	3	WEEKS		550	1,650	
	WRAP	1	WEEK		0	0	2,450
2021	Second Assist. Directors						
	PREP	1	WEEK	0.60	300	180	
	SHOOT	3	WEEKS		350	1,050	
	WRAP	1	WEEK		0	0	1,230
2029	DGA Trainee						0
2031	Script Supervisors						
	PREP	1	WEEK	0.20	500	100	
	SHOOT	3	WEEKS		500	1,500	
	WRAP	1	WEEK	0.20	500	100	1,700
2032	Technical Advisors						0
2032	Production Coordinator						
	PREP	2	WEEKS		300	600	
	SHOOT	3	WEEKS		350	1,050	
	WRAP	1	WEEK		300	300	1,950
2035	Production Secretary						0
2037	Production Assistant(s)						
		25	DAYS		60	1,500	
		20	DAYS		50	1,000	2,500
2041	Choreographer(s)						0
2061	Standby First Aid	2	DAYS		250	500	500
2071	Welfare Worker(s)						0
2081	Production Accountant(s)						
	PREP	2	WEEKS	0.50	500	500	
	SHOOT	3	WEEKS		500	1,500	
	WRAP	1	WEEK		500	500	2,500
2084	Additional Hire						0
2085	Other Charges						0
						Total for 2000	15,980

Production Staff

On big-budget shows, the days of the lean production staff may be gone forever. While not even the Directors Guild has raised their minimum staffing beyond the basic Unit Production Manager, First Assistant Director, and Second Assistant Director, legions of production people are not unusual. Your micro-budget enterprise can't afford much more than the "minimum staffing" and, unless you have a lot of cast or extras, should not *need* more than that. The rates here are typical for micro-budget. Remember, people who are looking for days that count toward the "qualification lists" that restrict those who may be hired on DGA shows are getting more than a salary from you, they're getting a career boost.

You can supplement (or reduce) your paid staff in this category or any other below-the-line category by using "Interns," i.e., unpaid apprentices. Remember, people who work without pay, however low their rate, have no motivation other than the experience for staying on. Just that experience is reward enough for the star struck and the reel builders, but if people aren't treated well, they may quickly decide to stop coming back for more.

As per our comment in the first paragraph, you may find it easier to hire $50-a-day Production Assistants, if you agree to call them Second Second Assistant Directors.

Our sample show, *Desire Under the Magnolias*, has no children working and the only stunt is a fist fight. Consequently, there are no Welfare Workers budgeted, and Standby First Aid will only be used on a daily basis for the fight scenes. Obviously, micro-budgeteers do not have the resources to support large action scripts from any standpoint: time, material (trashing cars and blowing things up creates debris), and especially safety. Some of the new posting requirements regarding Occupational Safety and Health may seem inappropriate to the temporary nature of the independent production unit, but the underlying safety concern is entirely valid. The bottom line is just don't try a stunt or a special effect that you cannot afford to stage safely. In the final analysis, fines and lawsuits are a lot costlier than savings on safety personnel or equipment.

Acct #	Description	Amount	Units	X	Rate	Subtotal	Total
2100	**Extra Talent**						
2101	Stand-ins						
	Stand-ins (Non-SAG)	15	DAYS	2	50	1,500	1,500
2103	Extras						
	Extras	50	DAYS		65	3,250	3,250
2105	Crowds Extras	200	DAYS		45	9,000	9,000
2107	Dancers, Skaters, etc.						0
2121	Teachers, Welfare Workers						0
2123	Interviews & Transport.						0
2125	Atmosphere Cars						0
2181	Casting Fees - Extras	13,750	%	0.08	1	1,100	1,100
2185	Other Charges						0
					Total for 2100		14,850

Extra Talent

In non-SAG micro-budget shows, actors typically earn from zero to $75 per day. Since SAG took over West Coast representation of all "on-camera performers" several years ago, the base rate for Extras (i.e., on-camera performers who utter no meaningful sounds) has been $65 per day.

Stand-ins are $90.

Do you even need stand-ins on a micro-budget? Sure, they're useful but not absolutely necessary. You can buy, process, and print several hundred feet of film for the daily cost of a stand-in including fringes. And while the SAG contract requires everyone photographed to be either Actor or Extra, there are no minimum number of stand-ins required. Rather than argue with SAG, for the time being at least, they will gladly negotiate any low-budget deal, and they will actually take your total budget into account. The assumption in the sample budget is a typical one: non-SAG stand-ins or no stand-ins are required, but you must pay fifty man-days of SAG extras over the course of the production. Even on normal-budget shows, where SAG permits non-members to be used after a cut-off point of union-hires, "Crowd Extras" designate non-SAG performers.

If a scene requires specialty wardrobes or cars, SAG extras are paid an additional allowance. But these amounts are still cheaper than renting your own wardrobe or atmosphere cars. There are also payments and conditions covering everything from interviews to mileage allowances.

The easiest way to deal with extras is to use a casting service. Even the world-famous Central Casting can provide SAG and non-SAG performers to your specifications. Of course, this is for a fee. These are all negotiable, and the rate entered here is at the lower end of the scale.

Acct #	Description	Amount	Units	X	Rate	Subtotal	Total
2200	**Art Direction**						
2201	Production Designer						
	PREP	2	WEEKS		600	1,200	
	SHOOT	3	WEEKS		600	1,800	
	WRAP	1	WEEK		600	600	3,600
2211	Art Director						0
2215	Assistant Art Director						0
2217	Set Const. Coordinator						0
2219	Set Designers & Draftsman						0
2221	Model Makers						0
2231	Sketch Artists						0
2241	Set Estimators						0
2261	Materials						0
2271	Purchases						0
2285	Other Charges						0
					Total for 2200		3,600

Art Direction

We are now entering the Twilight Zones of micro-budget. The cost of everything that has to do with Production, both material and technical staff, can vary over a wide range. Need an expensive prop (or expensive anything) that you can't afford? You have a range of alternatives restricted only by your imagination. From rewriting to reconstructing, there are ways other than cash to get what you need.

One thing you must have (unless you plan on doing every job yourself) is someone in charge of the Art Department. Getting an experienced Production Designer/Art Director (or any department head) for a micro-budget wage is only half of the problem. What you really need is someone who can squeeze the other people and material out of those few pennies left over after his or her own salary is paid. In some cases, you can make an "all-in" deal with some department heads, such as the production designer or the special-effects foreman, to simply provide everything that the script requires for a fixed, total fee. If you do, remember that this invites people to really cut costs, because they keep whatever is left over. The result may be not just cheap but cheap looking, too.

You can budget a package amount for the entire Art Department, including Set Dressing and Props in this category. It is more typical, however, to break those down in the accounts that follow.

Acct #	Description	Amount	Units	X	Rate	Subtotal	Total
2300	**Set Construction**						
2301	Set Const. - Payroll						0
2302	Set Const. - Materials						0
	Set Const. - Purchases						0
	Set Const. - Rentals						0
2303	Electric Scaffolding						0
						Total for 2300	0
2400	**Set Striking**						
2401	Set Striking						0
						Total for 2400	0

Set Construction

Here's another empty page. You're probably wondering by now why you paid good money for a book full of so many zeroes. We could just leave these out. Don't computer budgets have an option that omits empty accounts when it's time to print? As we've said, part of the process is knowing what you don't have. Even on a micro-budget, there may be a time when it is cheaper to build a set than to find a practical location.

If you are budgeting Set Construction, remember that the bare walls are nothing more than a few painted flats, which can usually be rented from studio scene dock. The real expense will likely be in the furniture, drapes, and carpets that even an ordinary room requires for realistic appearance.

Set Striking

If you build it, then the strikers (guys with hammers not baseball bats) will come to take it down. Even normal-budget shows usually contract for constructing *and* striking in one package.

Acct #	Description	Amount	Units	X	Rate	Subtotal	Total
2500	**Set Operations**						
2501	Key Grip						
	PREP	1	WEEK	0.60	600	360	
	SHOOT	3	WEEKS		600	1,800	
	WRAP	1	WEEK	0.20	600	120	2,280
2511	2nd Grip						0
2515	Dolly Grip						
	PREP	1	WEEK	0.20	550	110	
	SHOOT	3	WEEKS		550	1,650	
	WRAP	1	WEEK	0.20	0	0	1,760
2517	Crane Operators						0
2519	Grips						
	PREP	2	WEEKS	0.20	400	160	
	SHOOT	3	WEEKS		400	1,200	
	WRAP	1	WEEK	0.20	400	80	1,440
2521	Greensman						0
2523	Painters						0
2531	Craft Service Person(s)						
	PREP	1	WEEK	0.20	350	70	
	SHOOT	3	WEEKS		350	1,050	
	WRAP	1	WEEK	0.20	350	70	1,190
2537	Set Laborer(s)						0
2541	Grip Equipment - Studio						0
2545	- Location	2	WEEKS		500	1,000	1,000
2551	Purchases						0
2555	Condor(s)						0
2557	Dolly Rental						0
2559	Crane Rental						0
2561	Camera Platforms						0
2565	Car Mounts						0
2571	Expendables		Allow		1,500	1,500	1,500
2581	Box Rentals						0
2585	Other Charges						0
					Total for 2500		9,170

Set Operations

For micro-budgeting purposes, this account covers the Grip Department and Craft Service. If you feel the need for a Greensman or a standby Painter, you might want to reconsider (a) your approach or (b) your script. Seriously, you will always need a Grip or two, but the rest of the labor in this account is optional.

This sample has three grips, as it will be shot on practical locations where windows will have to be blacked out or covered with gel and day exteriors will be lit by reflectors. We expect these and other tasks to be accomplished by a lighting crew complement of seven Grips and Electricians, none of whom will be highly paid. The alternate approach would be fewer (four or five total) people paid more money, which is equally valid for micro-budgeteers.

Avoid "sweetheart deals." If you give some of the crew more salary than their interdepartmental peers and word gets out, you risk major disgruntlement on the part of the lower-paid. Like actors, crew have a lot of time between takes to stand around and talk to each other, and money is a subject close to their hearts. "Favored nations" or equal pay for equal work is a great concept that can give you a lot of dealmaking leverage. If you must pay some people more, call it an additional "box rental" or some sort of allowance and make sure they are sworn to secrecy.

We've also budgeted a Craft Service person, whom we will consider a Technical P.A., capable not just of buying donuts on the way in and brewing some coffee but assisting any department that may need some spot help. On a micro-budget, everyone from the Producer on down should know the business end of a C-stand and how to coil electrical cable.

Acct #	Description	Amount	Units	X	Rate	Subtotal	Total
2600	**Special Effects**						
2601	Foremen						0
2602	Other Effectsmen						0
2603	Rigging-Effects & Explos.						0
2604	Effects - Striking						0
2605	Other Deptartment Labor						0
2606	Materials						0
2607	Purchases						0
2608	Rentals						0
	Effects Boxes						0
2685	Other Charges						0
						Total for 2600	0

Special Effects

Yet another empty category. Just to balance out, we won't write much on this side of the page either. Our basic advice is don't even try to blow anything up on a micro-budget. Get some good actors, make an art film. That's going to make a bigger impression than some hazardous-to-shoot, cheap-looking explosions. If you feel that you have to put an explosion on your key art, go ahead. Buy some stock shots of building demolitions and stick them into your title sequence. It's faster, cheaper, and safer.

The other mechanical effects that the union world reserves for a specialist, such as elevator doors opening or indicator lights flashing on a telephone, can almost always be handled by others on the crew.

Acct #	Description	Amount	Units	X	Rate	Subtotal	Total
2700	**Set Dressing**						
2701	Set Decorator						
	PREP	2	WEEKS		500	1,000	
	SHOOT	3	WEEKS		500	1,500	
	WRAP	1	WEEK	0.60	500	300	2,800
2711	On-Set Dresser						0
2721	Lead Person						0
2725	Swing Crew						
	Allow	7	DAYS		65	455	455
2727	Extra Swing Crew						0
2745	Draperies						0
2747	Manufacturing Labor						0
2751	Purchases		Allow		1,500	1,500	1,500
2761	Rentals		Allow		2,000	2,000	2,000
2781	Box Rentals						0
2783	Repairs & Damages		Allow		500	500	500
2785	Other Charges						0
					Total for 2700		7,255

Set Dressing

As we said earlier, Set Dressing is the key to a realistic look. On the other hand, we are talking about the type of furnishings that everyone has in their home and that is already in place at most locations. Micro-budgeteers need to get the maximum impact out of what comes with a rental and what they may already have elsewhere. A knowledgeable Set Decorator or Dresser can take you a long way toward accomplishing this goal, which is why the labor cost here is almost equal to the amount that's been allowed for rentals and purchases. We'd make some smart comment about the party animals on the Swing Crew, but these are burly guys who come in to move furniture on and off the truck, and they could drop something the next time we work.

If, in fact, there are no "special items" whatsoever called for in your script, you may be able to get by with even less. But you still need someone in charge of making sure the sets on any and all locations are ready to shoot when you get there. Where a standard budget would call for a dressing crew of three, four, or five people and a couple of trucks to haul furniture in, you can get by with one person with his or her own pickup and some day help the other end of the heavy items.

Acct #	Description	Amount	Units	X	Rate	Subtotal	Total
2800	**Property**						
	Property Shooting Co.						0
2801	Property Master						
	PREP	1	WEEK		500	500	
	SHOOT	2	WEEKS		500	1,000	
	WRAP	1	WEEK	0.60	500	300	1,800
2803	Assistant Property Master						
	Allow	10	DAYS		65	650	650
2805	3rd Property Man						0
2811	Animal Handlers-Trainers						0
2821	Animals						0
2831	Purchases		Allow		750	750	750
	Rentals						0
2841	General		Allow		1,000	1,000	1,000
2845	Special Items						0
2849	Ammunition & Explosives						0
2851	Expendables						0
2881	Box Rentals						0
2883	Loss and Damage		Allow		500	500	500
2885	Other Charges						0
					Total for 2800		4,700

38

Property

We're tempted to just write "ditto" here. One sharp person working props is better than a phalanx of inexperienced P.A.s. But don't expect one person to be in two places at once. Props are rented by the day, week, or month; and a single prop person can't be picking up an item the day before you need it or getting it off rental as soon as you're done with it *and* standing by on the set at all times, too. So we've allowed a few days of a prop P.A., who hopefully owns a van or a pickup, also, to take care of carting items back and forth.

On micro-budget shows, the total Rental and Purchases allowances for both Set Dressing and Property should be considered interchangeable. The breakdowns here are arbitrary, and you can combine them into one account for both departments. If the Production Designer/Art Director is not assuming the overall responsibility for making sure the budgeted amounts are not exceeded, then it may make sense to have separate accounts with someone in each department keeping track or a designated supervisor of consolidated accounts.

Before you look at your script and decide that it doesn't have any props, remember that it's not just a question of guns or pogo sticks. Everyday items from address books and answering machines to wallets and wristwatches (we couldn't think of one—let alone two—everyday items that started with "Z," okay) become props if an actor uses them. And if you're thinking of trusting an actor to bring matching clothes and accessories with him or her every day, then you haven't worked with actors before.

Acct #	Description	Amount	Units	X	Rate	Subtotal	Total
2900	**Men's Wardrobe**						
2901	Costume Designer						0
2903	Wardrobe Supervisor						
	PREP	1	WEEK		500	500	
	SHOOT	3	WEEKS		500	1,500	
	WRAP	1	WEEK	0.20	500	100	2,100
2905	1st Men's Wardrobe						0
2907	2nd Men's Wardrobe						0
2909	Local Labor						0
2911	Wardrobe Manufacturing						0
2921	Wardrobe Purchases		Allow		1,000	1,000	1,000
2931	Wardrobe Rentals	1			250	250	250
2941	Wardrobe Cleaning		Allow		750	750	750
2981	Wardrobe Damages						
			Allow		250	250	250
2983	Box Rentals						0
2985	Other Charges						0
					Total for 2900		4,350

Men's Wardrobe

Despite that last bon mot under Property, you may want to use the Actor's own clothes. Just make sure that you put a Wardrobe person in charge of them. Yes, you guessed it, as with previous departments, the Costumers, or "rag pickers" as they are affectionately known, are more important than the dollar amount of Rentals and Purchases. Whether you use an actor's own clothes and/or buy and rent them, someone has to coordinate this. This means not only making sure they get to the set the first time, but every time.

As with Set Dressing and Props, it is not possible to be working the set and picking up or returning items at the same time. *Desire Under the Magnolias,* our prototype, has limited cast and limited wardrobe requirements. Most of the cast will wear their own. That's why cleaning is more than a third of the total material budget. We've put both men's and women's Purchases and Rentals into a single account; but, so it won't be yet another empty category, we've put the wardrobe assistant at a P.A. rate into the next account.

Acct #	Description	Amount	Units	X	Rate	Subtotal	Total
3000	**Women's Wardrobe**						
3001	Costume Designer						0
3003	Wardrobe Supervisor						0
3005	1st Women's Wardrobe						
	PREP	1	DAY		60	60	
	SHOOT	3	WEEKS		300	900	
	WRAP	1	DAY		60	60	1,020
3007	2nd Women's Wardrobe						0
	Local Labor						0
	Wardrobe Manufacturing						0
	Wardrobe Purchases						0
	Wardrobe Rentals						0
	Wardrobe Cleaning						0
	Wardrobe Damages						0
	Box Rentals						0
	Other Charges						0
							0
	INCLUDED IN ACCOUNT 2900						0
						Total for 3000	1,020

Women's Wardrobe

As noted above, a Wardrobe P.A. is budgeted here for one prep day, the shooting days, and one wrap day. As with Set Dressing and Props, the assumption is that someone who wants to build up a résumé in the craft of their choice will work at a P.A. rate for a technical credit. Like all our assumptions, this one is, of course, based on our practical experience and vast knowledge of the micro-budget world. If you want to strike a blow against the industry sexism that's built into a budget form that refers to many crew persons as "man," you can reverse this and put the wardrobe supervisor in this account and the P.A. in men's wardrobe.

Small cast, you say. Why not just have one costumer? If there aren't a lot of pick-ups and returns, like the prop or set dressing departments have, you could conceivably get by with one experienced costumer.

Just when we thought we couldn't vamp anymore in this account, we noticed the Box Rental category, empty and forlorn like all the rest in this sample budget. There are many departments where a Box Rental is not just an alternative to taxable salary. From a costumer's sewing kit to a craft-service person's cooler, experienced crew will be expected to have certain equipment. In the micro-budget world, you won't be expected to pay for them, but you should make that clear up front. And if something breaks, it's always a gesture of good faith to replace it. That's why there are Loss and Damage allowances in most departments.

Acct #	Description	Amount	Units	X	Rate	Subtotal	Total
3100	**Makeup & Hairdressing**						
3101	Makeup Supervisor						
	PREP	1	WEEK	0.20	600	120	
	SHOOT	3	WEEKS		600	1,800	
	WRAP	1	WEEK		600	0	1,920
3103	2nd Makeup Artist						0
3105	Additional Labor						0
	Hair Stylists						0
3111	Hairdressing Supervisor						
	PREP	1	WEEK	0.20	500	100	
	SHOOT	3	WEEKS		500	1,500	
	WRAP	1	WEEK		500	0	1,600
3113	2nd Hairstylist						0
3113	Additional Labor						0
3121	Body Makeup						0
3131	Purchases		Allow		500	500	500
3133	Appliances Mfg.						0
3141	Rentals						0
	Box Rentals-Makeup						0
	Box Rentals-Hair Stylists						0
3151	Purchases - Hair Pieces						0
	Wigs - Falls - etc.						0
3153	Rentals - Hair Pieces						0
	Wigs - Falls - etc.						0
3185	Other Charges						0
						Total for 3100	4,020

Makeup & Hairdressing

The exception that proves the rule (where do all these clichés come from? We're getting too old to check the compact *O.E.D.* without a magnifying glass): no Loss/Damage but an amount for Purchases that will cover such expendables as applicator sponges and hair spray. $500 may seem like a lot, but unless your cast is quite small, that's a typical amount.

Since the run-of-the-show cast is relatively small, we were tempted (we're being rhetorical here, of course, since *Desire Under the Magnolias* doesn't exist and we can decide anything we want) to budget one combination Makeup/Hair person. Most practitioners can perform both functions, and even at a slight premium, one person is obviously cheaper than two. Since a lot of scenes involved two female performers at the beginning of the day, rather than risk losing even half an hour of production time per day waiting for them, the decision was to budget for two people in this department.

Acct #	Description	Amount	Units	X	Rate	Subtotal	Total
3200	**Elec., Rigging & Oper.**						
	Lighting Shooting Co.						0
3201	Gaffer						
	PREP	1	WEEK	0.60	600	360	
	SHOOT	3	WEEKS		600	1,800	
	WRAP	1	WEEK	0.20	600	120	2,280
3211	Best Boy						
	PREP	1	WEEK	0.20	500	100	
	SHOOT	3	WEEKS		500	1,500	
	WRAP	1	WEEK	0.20	500	100	1,700
3221	Elect. Operators - Labor						
	PREP	1	WEEK	0.20	400	80	
	SHOOT	3	WEEKS	2	400	2,400	
	WRAP	1	WEEK	0.20	400	80	2,560
3231	Generator Operator						0
3241	Wind Machine Operator						0
3245	Local Elect. Operators						0
3251	Electrical Equipment						
	Package	3	WEEKS		1,500	4,500	4,500
3265	Globes and Expendables						
	Included Above Acct. 2571						0
3271	Repairs						0
3275	Generator Rentals						
	Included Below Acct. 3531						0
3277	Fuel (Generators)						
	Included Below Acct. 3581						0
3279	Purchases						0
3281	Box Rentals						0
3283	Loss/Damage		Allow		500	500	500
3285	Other Charges						0
						Total for 3200	11,540

Electrical, Rigging & Operator

As we noted under Set Operations, there are four people in this department (the 2 in the "X" column of Account 3221 indicates the second lamp operator for the shooting period). Since there is no exterior night photography, it might have been possible to get by with less. Again, the overriding consideration should be the production hours. With only fifteen total days, $1,200 for a fourth person in this department is a cheap hedge against lost time. Also remember that most departments will work better if they are not underpaid *and* understaffed. As we noted in the last account, combining jobs also implies a premium rate.

The basic Electrical package will probably come from the same supplier as the Grip package, and it may also include the Production Van, which is budgeted under Transportation. You can combine all three items into a single line item. If you do so, since the Electrical Package will be the costliest element, you should put that Package allowance in this account.

We have not detailed out the Generator, which should be part of the Production Van rental, or the Fuel, which will be part of the same line item in Transportation. As in the sample, you may want to include annotations that make it clear that you have not forgotten about these items

The Expendables for Grip and Electric can be quite costly, particularly rolls of neutral-density and color-correcting gel. Several outlets sell the equivalent of the "short ends," and many Key Grips and Gaffers will have items stashed in their garages, out of which they should be cajoled.

Acct #	Description	Amount	Units	X	Rate	Subtotal	Total
3300	**Camera Operations**						
3301	Director of Photography						
	PREP	1	WEEK	0.50	1,000	500	
	SHOOT	3	WEEKS		1,000	3,000	
	WRAP	1	WEEK		1,000	0	3,500
3311	Camera Operator(s)						0
3321	Camera Assistant(s)						
	1st Assistant						
	PREP	1	WEEK	0.40	500	200	
	SHOOT	3	WEEKS		600	1,800	
	WRAP	1	WEEK	0.20	500	100	
	2nd Assistant						
	PREP	1	WEEK	0.20	300	60	
	SHOOT	3	WEEKS		350	1,050	
	WRAP	1	WEEK	0.20	300	60	3,270
3331	Loader(s)						0
3341	Still Photographer		Allow		1,200	1,200	1,200
3351	Camera Package	3	WEEKS		2,250	6,750	6,750
3361	Expendables		Allow		500	500	500
3371	Special Equipment						0
3381	Box Rentals						0
3385	Other Charges						0
					Total for 3300		15,220

Camera Operations

The Director of Photography is the most important below-the-line person and should be compensated accordingly. This is a micro-budget salary, but it's still more than anyone else is making, and it should be. With this sum, you need the best and fastest D.P. that you can find. Getting somebody at a great rate won't help you if that person can't perform at the required pace. A D.P. who will work for less but needs twenty days to photograph your micro-budget endeavor is obviously a bad choice. At this budget level, you will expect the D.P. to operate the camera as well and to have a total crew of three persons, including the D.P., rather than the four mandated under union conditions.

The Camera package is also a key element. In *Hollywood on $5,000, $10,000, or $25,000 a Day,* we wrote that some micro-budgeteers have rented a Panaflex Gold package with prime lenses and zoom, batteries, mags, sticks, Sachler head, all of it for $1,600 a week. But, although these were real deals, they are strictly no quote, so don't expect to fax a copy of this to someone at Panavision and get the same deal. So what deal can you get? If you are willing to use less than the latest, has-all-the-bells-and-whistles-which-you-won't-use-anyway model of any camera (an Arri BL II or III or a Panaflex-X), the prices in the printed rate book will fall dramatically. If you are renting cameras, or any equipment, at times when fewer other shows are shooting (late Spring and early Summer) and vendors have more equipment in stock, prices are more flexible. To a supplier, some dollars a week is better than zero dollars a week for equipment that otherwise would be sitting on the shelf.

As stills are usually part of any delivery deal, ideally the Still Photographer should be on the set every day. A typical compromise on a micro-budget is to hire someone on a package-fee basis for a fixed amount that covers a negotiated number of days on the set covering key scenes and actors.

Acct #	Description	Amount	Units	X	Rate	Subtotal	Total
3400	**Sound Operations**						
3401	Sound Mixer						
	Package (includes Nagra)	3	WEEKS		1,750	5,250	5,250
3411	Boom Person	3	WEEKS		450	1,350	1,350
3415	Sound Utility						0
3417	Playback Operator(s)						0
3402	Purchases						0
3421	1/4" Magnetic Tape		Allow		500	500	500
	Rentals						0
3431	Sound Channel						0
3441	Walkie Talkies						0
3451	Special Equipment						0
3452	Playback						0
3483	Equipment Repairs		Allow		250	250	250
3485	Other Charges						0
					Total for 3400		7,350

Sound Operations

While it is true that bad sound can be looped or otherwise replaced later and bad picture cannot, a good production track saves time and money in post. Lest it seem that we have immediately violated our maxim about the D.P. and paid the Mixer more, note that the weekly rate includes the Sound Channel (annotated because of space limitations on the budget form as "Nagra"). For the rate, we would expect not only a Nagra but wireless microphones, fishpole boom, cables, connectors, etc. The ideal would be a time-code-based Nagra, but that alone would rent for $750 to $1,000 per week from equipment vendors. If you plan on cutting on Avid or D-Vision (as is assumed in this sample) or some other non-linear system, however, the time-code Nagra or a time-code DAT recorder is required.

We're not using Nagra as a synonym for a portable sound recorder because we own stock in Nagra or because there are no alternate digital recorders available, but because the sheer number of Nagras in use makes it unlikely that a micro-budget show will be recording production sound with anything else. As with cameras, an older Nagra model may prove a reliable, cut-rate alternative. Whatever the recording device, in addition to the 1/4-inch tape or DAT cassettes to record on, there are other expendables, most notably batteries. You can add a line item for these, or just figure them into the tape allowance.

Acct #	Description	Amount	Units	X	Rate	Subtotal	Total
3500	**Transportation**						
3501	Trans. Coordinator						
	PREP	2	WEEKS		600	1,200	
	SHOOT	3	WEEKS		600	1,800	
	WRAP	1	WEEK	0.60	600	360	3,360
3503	Driver Captain						0
3505	Driver Co-Captain						0
3511	Drivers						
	PREP	1	WEEK	0.40	400	160	
	SHOOT	3	WEEKS	2	400	2,400	
	WRAP	1	WEEK	0.40	400	160	2,720
3531	Vehicle Rentals						
	Production Van w. Gen.	3	WEEKS		950	2,850	
	Camera/Sound Van	3	WEEKS		425	1,275	
	Prop/set Van	2	WEEKS		325	650	
		3	WEEKS		325	975	
		1	WEEK	0.40	325	130	
	Makeup/Wardrobe Trailer	2	WEEKS	0.40	325	260	
		3	WEEKS		325	975	
		1	WEEK	0.20	325	65	7,180
3551	Dressing Room Rentals						
	Honeywagon (incl. Driver)	3	WEEKS		1,700	5,100	5,100
3571	Picture Cars						
			Allow		750	750	750
3581	Fuel		Allow		4,500	4,500	4,500
3583	Repairs and Maintenance		Allow		500	500	500
3584	Mileage Allowance						0
3585	Other Charges						0
					Total for 3500		24,110

Transportation

The next two departments represent the greatest challenge for micro-budgeteers. While the estimated costs are small in the great scheme of moviemaking, they are a significant portion of this sample budget and could still easily prove inadequate.

Lurking in the background of most L.A.-based shows are a couple of tough-talking union organizers who will want you to sign with the Teamsters. They will regularly check public records, such as filming permits, to try and hunt down your ilk. If these guys find your location, you might want to show them your budget. It won't make them go away, but it might make them think twice about bothering to throw up a picket line.

Times are tough in Tinsel Town, so much so that you might even be able to find a Teamster to work for the sub-standard wages your micro-budget allows. Whoever you hire to coordinate transportation should, like his or her department-head peers, be familiar with the low-budget alternatives. There are, for instance, Honeywagons with five or more rooms that can be found for even less than the amount budgeted here (including driver), but that are not 1995 models with lots of shiny chrome. The same is true of all the rolling stock. The assumption has been that other departments will "drive their own," which can work with smaller trucks and vans; items such a production vans and wardrobe trailers require drivers with commercial licenses to operate them.

Other often-overlooked problems include the fact that *micro*-budgeteers and *large* vehicles are antonymic and don't mix very well. Once you manage to rent these oversized, multi-wheeled wagons and find street-legal drivers, you still have to fuel them and post the streets at your location so that you'll have someplace to park them while you work and find some other, reasonably secure place half the size of a train yard to stash them overnight. And if you wonder why we've included all of two drivers in this cut-rate budget, remember that besides driving these vehicles from one location to another, the loss and damage charges are usually lower if someone actually stays with them while you shoot. If you are not using SAG actors, or even if you are, you can fudge a bit with the requirement of giving each performer his or her own room. But don't expect union or non-union actors to change clothes behind the bushes or in a closet. A reasonable place to wait will enhance many performances.

Lest you think this will be your most troublesome category, let's move on.

Location

More trouble. Fortunately, *Desire Under the Magnolias* takes place on a run-down ranch and a few urban locations, so maybe we would get it done for what's estimated here.

Let's go right to the key categories. They're the ones that stand out because their totals are five digits wide:

Meals and Site Rentals. The first is pretty self-explanatory. No matter how little pay folks will settle for, it's well nigh impossible to get them to bring a lunch box. Besides, while sitting under those magnolias, swatting flies and downing Salisbury steak, the morning's work will be reviewed and the chances for getting the rest of your scheduled scenes shot that afternoon will be carefully weighed. You have to feed your cast and crew. You can get box lunches or cook up your own for less than $11 a head. You can find caterers who transport chafing dishes in the trunk of their cars and might charge a dollar or two less; but a decent meal has a significant physical and psychological impact. Those carbos will sustain people in the afternoon when they start to run down. And, if it's a good meal, the anticipation of sitting down to eat real food will get people through the morning a lot better than donuts.

Site Rentals are one of the most treacherous line items on any micro-budget. It's not a bad idea to have done some scout-

Acct #	Description	Amount	Units	X	Rate	Subtotal	Total
3600	**Location**						
3601	Location Manager(s)						
		2	WEEKS		500	1,000	
		3	WEEKS		500	1,500	
		1	WEEK		500	0	2,500
3611	Police/Fire Personnel						
			Allow		3,000	3,000	
	Security		Allow		900	900	3,900
3621	Meals						
		15	DAYS	60	11	9,900	
	Extra Meals		Allow		1,500	1,500	11,400
3631	Site Rentals	15	DAYS		1,000	15,000	15,000
3641	Travel/Accommodations						0
3645	Courtesy Payments						0
3651	Custom Fees, Duties, etc.						0
3653	Film Shipment						0
3655	Foreign Travel Permits						0
3657	Flight Insurance						0
3661	Location Scouting						0
3671	Location Contact						0
3683	Loss and Damage		Allow		1,000	1,000	1,000
3685	Other Charges						0
					Total for 3600		33,800

ing of locations before you even make the budget. It's a good thing to do before you even write the script. But if you haven't, then be prepared for a lot of compromises or a lot of overages. It's not just people in Los Angeles (or other L.A.-area municipalities) who are hip to location fees, want more money, and to be named as "additional insureds" on a million-dollar liability policy. Thanks to *Entertainment Tonight* and all its clones, people everywhere hear that a movie company's coming and get those cartoon-character dollar signs in their eyes. When you figure that it includes permits, payoffs to neighbors, loss or damage, and supplementary sites as needed to park crew cars or set up lunch tables, $1,000 per day is not a high average. It won't buy you a lot of mansions or run-down ranch houses, or even ordinary tract homes. It won't let you shoot in such inhospitably high-priced precincts as Beverly Hills, Pasadena, or Torrance. "Torrance?" you say. Think of it as Palos Verdes-adjacent. Go to El Monte instead. Another thing that puts some municipalities out of your price range is the number of standby police and fire personnel they require you to hire. Keep these hidden costs in mind when you choose locations.

Unless you want to arrange all these details yourself, or overburden your already-busy production manager, an experienced location manager is essential.

Production Film & Laboratory

Just when you thought you were over the budgetary hump, here comes the largest account of all. You've got to have film; and if you don't process it and print it (either on film or video), it's going to be awfully hard to see the results. We talked about film and shooting ratios in the Introduction; here's where that translates to dollars and cents.

As we said in our last book, fresh stock from Kodak including sales tax is almost fifty cents per foot. No matter how you factor it, when that stuff is going through the camera at 90 feet per minute, you can't help but hear a cash register somewhere going "ca-ching" over and over again. What do you do to avoid going comatose from sticker shock? Some people are using video. They flip that "film look" switch on their Betacams and hope no one will notice. That may work for porno films, but not if you're making a micro-budget feature *film.* Note the italicized word.

So how do you get cheap film? The strategy is the same for all "expendable" items. Half a roll of gel is less than half price, so is half a roll of film. There are several companies that specialize in selling used film. They have everything from full cans that others bought but never got around to opening to those hundred-foot leftovers from a thousand-foot roll. Cut out the middleman. Track down other micro-budgeteers and get their film for a little as possible. Even if you split the difference between what a raw-stock exchange would pay them and then would charge you, you can sometimes get from almost four bits a foot for fresh from Kodak all the way down to two bits. That's almost twice as much film or half as much money.

There are other alternatives. As you'll hear from Mark Pirro in Part Two, Pirromount Pictures has most often used a considerably smaller gauge than 35mm. But even on a micro-budget, 35mm is the standard format.

Should you cut on film or tape? In this budget, we've got money for a rock-bottom "Avid-style" video cut. Initially this will

Acct #	Description	Amount	Units	X	Rate	Subtotal	Total
3700	**Prod. Film & Laboratory**						
3701	Picture Negative	45,000	FEET		0.37	16,650	16,650
3711	Film Processing						
	Includes video prep	45,000	FEET	0.90	0.13	5,265	5,265
3715	Normal Developing						
	AVID-style transfer	30	HOURS		275	8,250	8,250
3719	Forced Developing						0
3721	1 Light Dailies						0
3725	Timed Dailies						0
3731	Special Laboratory Work						0
3741	Stills-Negative & Lab.						0
3751	Sound Transfers Dailies						0
3753	Labor						0
3755	Mag. Stripe						0
3785	Other Charges						
	3/4 inch Video Stock	30	UNITS		12	360	360
					Total for 3700		30,525

cost more. "Printing" is twice as costly. Assuming you can get a lab to process and make a workprint from your negative for 20¢ per foot, that price will not permit you to "circle" or select takes. Subtracting the typical 10% allowed for waste from the total amount of negative, this means that you could make a film workprint of 90% of 45,000 feet for an effective cost of 7¢ a foot plus tax, or just over $3,000. That is a lot less than the $8,250 we have budgeted.

Where is this 7¢ in the budget? We're not making a workprint so it's not there. It's a hypothetical cost for comparison purposes. How do we arrive at this amount? In a deal to process and print film, the processing portion might well be less than the 13¢ a foot that we do have budgeted, but that's a pretty good price to process and "video prep" or get the negative *and* sound rolls ready for transfer to video. For comparison purposes, we've used the hypothetical 7¢, or the 20¢ that it would cost to process and print minus the 13¢ to process only, to get the effective cost of producing a workprint of all your negative. With Avid, D-Vision, or similar systems, you can transfer circled takes, which should, on average, add up to about 3,000 feet or 30 minutes a day. How does that equal the budgeted two hours (30 hours, 15 days) per day? Four-to-one is the minimum ratio of running time to transfer time for these systems. Remember that the lab is not just transferring negative but also synching up sound using the original Nagra rolls with time-code reference *and* making you a computer diskette of time code/edge number references that you will need to cut the negative. Six- or eight-to-one ratios are not uncommon.

Considering that a computer-based or "non-linear" digital system also costs a lot more to rent than a moviola, how do we justify the video cut decision? Didn't we write just last year in *Hollywood on $5,000, $10,000, or $25,000 a Day* that "cutting on film and mixing on tape will be the cheapest way to go"? Have we changed our minds? Have we lost our minds? You'll have to wait for Editing, Account 5000, to find out.

Acct #	Description	Amount	Units	X	Rate	Subtotal	Total
3800	**Stage Facilities**						
3801	Studio Stage Rental						0
3802	Distant Loc. Stage Rental						0
3803	Test Stage Rental						0
3804	Add. Studio Facilities						0
3805	Studio Personnel Required						0
3885	Other Charges						0
						Total for 3800	0
3900	**Process & Rear Projection**						
3901	Rear Projection						0
3985	Other Charges						0
						Total for 3900	0

Stage Facilities

Yes, we know, another blank page. Look at the bright side: We could have printed Accounts 3800 and 3900 on two separate blank pages. We didn't.

We already talked about shooting on Stages, which remains unlikely for micro-budgeteers unless there's a standing set of a courtroom or medical operating room or something that would be costly to rent as a practical. As we know, the bottom line is don't have any of these places in your script unless you know that you can get them for micro prices.

Process & Rear Projection

Process and Rear Projection? Remnants of a bygone era. It's time to drop these from the form. Or maybe we should substitute Blue Screen and Morphing. Either way, you can't afford any.

Acct #	Description	Amount	Units	X	Rate	Subtotal	Total
4000	**2nd Unit**						
4001	Production Staff						0
4002	Cast						0
4003	Extra Talent						0
4004	Set Construction						0
4005	Set Striking						0
4006	Set Operations						0
4007	Set Dressing						0
4008	Property						0
4009	Men's Wardrobe						0
4010	Women's Wardrobe						0
4011	Makeup & Hairdressing						0
4012	Electrical						0
4013	Camera						0
4014	Sound						0
4015	Special Effects						0
4016	Locations						0
4017	Transportation						0
4018	Purchases						0
4019	Rentals						0
4085	Other Charges						0
					Total for 4000		0

2nd Unit

While there is no 2nd Unit on *Desire Under the Magnolias*, it is not uncommon in micro-budget budgets. When you have a very short feature schedule, it makes sense to extract establishing shots and other MOS (if you don't know that it means "without sound," you need to bone up a bit more on production terms) moments. We and all our interviewees have used pre-production, simultaneous, and post-production 2nd Units to fill in the blanks. Since most camera packages should include a wild Arri (the hard-front version accommodates Panavision lenses), this un-blimped camera spends most of its rental time sitting in its box. It can often be outside on sticks shooting a wide shot of a building while you're inside dollying around some actors in an office. With just a smidgen of planning, you can even send the actors outside to be photographed entering and/or leaving the building. You don't really need to budget a simultaneous 2nd Unit to accomplish this. Just break off two or three people to set it up and do it.

You can also cajole or pay a reduced crew to drive around town with you on a Sunday or some other off day and use that rental equipment to grab a bunch of shots. A small, low-profile detachment can often accomplish this without benefit of location rentals, etc. In Los Angeles, a single permit can define several shooting areas geographically (i.e., bounded by four streets) and be good for a range of days. Remember, also, that if you can see something from a public thoroughfare such as a street or sidewalk, you don't need permission from the owner to photograph it. You can fill up a Sunday morning driving around and shooting out the side door of a van or even a car window, drive through you favorite fast-food franchise, and shoot some more till the sun goes down. Then shoot some expensive-looking night exteriors with the available light along Hollywood or some other well-lit boulevard.

Acct #	Description	Amount	Units	X	Rate	Subtotal	Total
4100	**Tests**						
4101	Tests		Allow		250	250	250
4185	Other Charges						0
						Total for 4100	250
4900	**Fringe Benefits**						
4999	Fringes						
	FICA	6.20	%		75,585	4,686	
	SUI/FUI	6.20	%		73,585	4,562	
	Medicare	1.45	%		75,585	1,096	
	Workers' Comp.	2.73	%		70,635	1,928	
	SAG - Extra	12.85	%		3,250	418	
	Payroll Charges	0.25	%		75,585	189	
	Sales Tax	8.25	%		51,025	4,210	
	Clerical Comp	0.79	%		4,450	35	17,124
						Total for 4900	17,124

Tests

Tests are cheap insurance. If you are renting a camera that's been knocked around for a few years, running a few feet of film through it to make sure everything's copacetic is a good practice.

Fringe Benefits

Here we are again at Fringes, which we will revisit twice more in Accounts 5900 and 7900. Computer budgets calculate Fringes automatically, and this form places them at the end of each major sub-section. Take a moment and look at the Fringes. If you bother to divide the sub-totals into the percentages, you will discover that they have been applied to different amounts of salary. That's because, as we said when we discussed above-the-line fringes, in a computer budget, you can quickly set up each fringe with its own cut-offs. We told you government fringe cut-offs and we didn't bore you with the SAG and other union fringes, since their cut-offs are at $200,000. For normal budgets, these union cut-offs should be factored in. There is no cut-off in Workmen's Comp, but a substantially lower rate is allowed for "clerical" employees (on the theory that they are significantly less at risk for an on-the-job injury), and we have tagged the Production Coordinator and Production Accountant at that rate. If you're doing the budget by hand, you may not think such fine distinctions are worthwhile, but as we said every penny counts in a micro-budget.

The total for this fringe category makes it your seventh largest account, and that may hardly seem like a "fringe" cost in the literal sense of the word. Do you really have to pay these? You certainly must pay the SAG fringes, even if you don't pay the salary! If you legally reduce the Fringes on the one hand by paying very small salaries and very large allowances, any dispute that ends up with the State Labor Board will quickly reveal that you didn't pay minimum wage for eight hours, let alone for overtime. You can defer the salaries and pay only allowances. If you do, be very careful of the wording of your deals or you still might end up with Social Security, IRS, and/or Labor Board problems. Whatever you do, whether you go through a payroll service or buy your own policy, don't fail to have Workmen's Comp, or someone else could end up owning your movie, your house, your first-born child, etc.

One last tip about Fringes: Payroll services are employers of record and work on calendar years. People working for you late in the year might already have reached or significantly approached the cut-offs for FICA, et al. on other shows. You can't count on this when you're budgeting, but if you're shooting in October, you can certainly ask people when you hire them if they've worked through a particular payroll service earlier in the year. If some of your crew have already earned over $7,000 or $60,000 through a particular official employer, which is what a payroll service is, and you hire them through that same official employer, there would be no more fringes on their earnings when they work on your show in the same calendar year. Consequently, using that same payroll service could conceivably save hundreds of dollars in fringe costs.

Production fringes also include Sales Tax. This should be applied to all rentals and to purchases such as film. You can apply sales tax to the allowances, also, or assume that tax is included, as is done in this sample budget. Even so, there is over $4,000 in sales tax in this sample, which is too large a sum to disregard when micro-budgeting. Some production companies try to get exemptions from sales tax by getting resale permits on the premise that they are renting and purchasing as part of the manufacturing process. Rules vary from state to state, and as many governing agencies hold that exemptions are restricted to items purchased for resale only, you should investigate before trying to use a resale permit to avoid sales tax. Past problems with audits have caused many Los Angeles purveyors, such as Panavision, to refuse to accept resale permits.

Editing

There is a sub-section of *Hollywood on $5,000, $10,000, or $25,000 a Day* called "Fixing It In Post," and before you make your decisions about which way to go, we suggest that it be read or, better yet, re-read.

Let's talk some more about film cut versus video cut and why an Avid-style cut is the choice for *Desire Under the Magnolias*. D-Vision is a simpler, more compact non-linear system than Avid, but it still costs a lot more to rent than a moviola. About twenty times more. But a film cut also requires an editing table, rewinds, bins, racks, splicers, split reels, synchronizers, and a room to work in. D-Vision requires a desk. Even so, all that mechanical equipment and a room are still a lot cheaper. The difference is time. Let's compare the numbers. The differences are spread over this account, Production Film & Lab, and Post Film & Lab:

	Film	Video
Printing	2,835	8,250
Video Stock	zero	360
Reprints/Coding/Reels/Leader, etc.	1,750	zero
Additional Sales Tax	zero	312
Editor (11.2 weeks vs. 7.2 weeks)	8,400	5,400
Assistant Editor (10.2 weeks @ 450)	4,500	zero
Additional Fringes	1,223	zero
Equipment Rental (11.2 weeks for Equipment & Room @ 350)	3,850	7,000
Negative Cut	4,000	5,000
Totals	**26,558**	**26,322**

Since the cost is almost the same, the key to our budgeting decision was efficiency. Is cutting on film that much slower? Would writing this book with a typewriter be slower than a personal computer? What do you think? Non-linear edits require less labor, but we are not assuming that salaries, which are al-

Acct #	Description	Amount	Units	X	Rate	Subtotal	Total
5000	**Editing**						
5001	Editor						
	PREP	1	WEEK	0.20	750	150	
	SHOOT	3	WEEKS		750	2,250	
	POST	4	WEEKS		750	3,000	5,400
5011	Assistant Editor(s)						0
5015	Apprentice Editor						0
5017	Additional Hire						0
5021	ADR Editor						0
5025	Sound Effects Editor						0
5031	Music Editor						0
5051	Projection (Prod./Editing						0
5055	Projection Location						0
5059	Film Messenger						0
5061	Cutting Rooms						0
5065	Equipment Rentals						
	D-Vision						
	PREP	0	WEEK		1,000	0	
	SHOOT	3	WEEKS		1,000	3,000	
	POST	4	WEEKS		1,000	4,000	7,000
5071	Purchases						0
5077	Coding						0
5083	Continuity Script						0
5085	Others Charges						0
					Total for 5000		12,400

ready quite cut-rate, could be lower. If anything, persons who are proficient on non-linear systems average higher salaries than those who can only drive a Kem.

Ultimately, the people involved in the process will be the critical components. When we wrote *Hollywood on $5,000, $10,000, or $25,000 a Day,* the number of Editors who had mastered the non-linear systems and would work for micro-budget rates was small. They're still not hordes of them out there, but the number has increased considerably, partly because the systems themselves are simpler. In our first book, we noted that David Lean cut *A Passage to India* himself on a moviola. That anecdote has a different implication now, as a lot of micro-budget directors would be open to a package deal that included doing his or her own editing on D-Vision. Some of these directors already own such a system. Non-linear cutting is faster, more compact, and produces a lot less physical trash. You don't need an assistant either to synch dailies or log trims. There are some drawbacks, the biggest being the quality of the digital video image. But the dailies on 3/4-inch will likely be just as good as a cheap (7¢!) workprint.

Acct #	Description	Amount	Units	X	Rate	Subtotal	Total
5100	**Music**						
5101	Composer/Conductor		ALLOW		7,500	7,500	7,500
5111	Musicians						0
5113	Arrangers						0
5115	Copyists						0
5117	Lyricist						0
5121	Coaches, Vocal Instructor						0
5131	Singers, Chorus						0
5141	Labor, Moving Instruments						0
5151	Synchronization License						0
5153	Recording Rights						0
5161	Music Re-use Fees						0
5171	Special Instrument Rental						0
5185	Other Charges						0
					Total for 5100		7,500

Music

Give an electronic wizard with some musical talent, whose den is packed with Macs and MIDIs, a chance with a time-coded 1/2-inch video of your picture and he or she will give you back an astonishing, digitally mastered underscore. And, if that wizard is someone with a lot of experience in commercials who wants to break into features, the price could be really low. The $7,500 in this budget is enough for someone with a few feature credits.

You may have heard about some new low-budget rates from the AFM. Or someone may have told you that you can get a big advance on the soundtrack rights from a record company and use that to pay for the score. To this we can only say, "Get real."

The same holds true for songs. We've worked on several features where we got songs for free from groups who have since gone on to Top 40 albums.

Choose your musical cohorts carefully. There will be plenty from which to choose. If there is any item that could cause almost as big a splash as throwing those scripts into the Pacific, it would be tossing in the demo cassettes in L.A. Of course, they have the disadvantage of being smaller and lighter than scripts.

Acct #	Description	Amount	Units	X	Rate	Subtotal	Total
5200	**Post Production Sound**						
5201	Transfer						0
5211	ADR Facilities						0
5215	Foley Facilities						0
5217	Scoring						0
5221	Music Dub Down						0
5223	Narration						0
5241	Temporary Dub						0
5243	Pre Dub						0
5251	Dubbing						
	24-track Package		Allow		17,500	17,500	17,500
5257	Magnetic Stock	10,000	FEET		0.08	800	800
5261	Music & Effects (Foreign)						0
5271	Other Purchases						0
5275	Rentals						0
5285	Other Charges						0
					Total for 5200		18,300

72

Post-Production Sound

Video facilities are not only smaller, faster, cleaner, and quieter than film facilities but astonishingly versatile. In slightly more time than it used to take to merely "spot" or plan out the sound effects, they can actually be laid in.

Package prices begin at $7,500 and go up from there, or so we said in our previous book. So why have we allowed more than twice that amount in this sample budget? Is there some unusually complex sound work required for *Desire Under the Magnolias*? No; but in the year since *Hollywood on $5,000, $10,000, or $25,000 a Day* was published, the rest of the world has discovered 24-track sound. There are more facilities than ever, and even more clients. Little rooms hidden away in dark corners of the San Fernando Valley must be booked months in advance, and many operate two shifts or even 24 hours a day almost the year around. With this kind of demand, even the new ones are less inclined to make someone a great deal to build up their client base. While these video mix-houses still require more than D-Vision's desk in the corner, it doesn't take many one-sheets from satisfied customers to cover the walls of their short hallways.

Acct #	Description	Amount	Units	X	Rate	Subtotal	Total
5300	**Post Prod. Film & Lab.**						
5301	Reprints - 1 light color						0
5305	B&W Reversal Work Prints						0
5311	Negative Cutting		Allow		5,000	5,000	5,000
5321	Answer Print	9,000	FEET		0.72	6,480	6,480
5331	Protective Mstr Positives						0
5335	Inter Negatives						0
5341	Optical Effects						0
5351	Optical Neg - Proc/print	9,000	FEET		0.32	2,880	2,880
5361	Process Plates						0
5363	Stock Footage						0
5371	Video Transfers						0
5375	One-inch Video Masters						0
5383	Shipping Charges						0
5385	Other Charges						0
					Total for 5300		14,360

Post-Production Film & Lab

Our assumption has been that you would be working toward a final version of your feature on film. Hence the costs budgeted here. You may have noticed in the cost comparisons in the text accompanying the editing account that there is a slight premium on cutting negative from the paper list generated by a non-linear system as opposed to the more traditional method of matching the edge numbers from a workprint. We're allowing 9,000 feet or approximately 100 minutes of final running time for the Answer Print. To make that composite 35mm print, you will also need to produce an optical soundtrack from your final mix.

This budget format does not detail, and we have not allowed, a licensing fee for either of the noise-reduction systems, Dolby or Ultra-Stereo. The process not only suppresses hiss but can encode multi-channel stereo in a center track. If you plan a theatrical release, using the less expensive Ultra system is recommended. You can negotiate the fee, with a low end of around $1,500. But there can be other costs, such as extra mix time or a company engineer for the transfer to the magnetic film master.

If you don't plan a theatrical release, you can skip the answer print altogether. You should still cut your negative and use that to produce a digital video master. An alternate method to get to a video master without cutting negative is to use the D-Vision analog source tapes—that is, the transfers from dailies—in a video on-line. If you use 3/4-inch tapes for the daily transfers, the resolution will not be as high as cutting the 35mm negative and transferring that, and the cost of an on-line will likely be greater than transferring to digital video from the cut negative. However you create a video master, you will not need an optical soundtrack, Dolby or Ultra, etc. You can simply lay over the master tracks from your mix.

If you are a little confused by these choices, there's more

detail in *Hollywood on $5,000*. Or check out this chart of comparables on how to get to a video master:

Costs	Answer Print	On-Line
To Final Picture (from above, less		
negative-cutting cost)	20,322	20,322
Negative Cut	5,000	—
On-Line Picture with Color Correction		
(16 hours @ $350)	—	5,600
Film Transfer with Color Correction		
(6 hours @ $450)	2,700	—
Lay-Over Audio (3 hours @ 150)	750	750
Totals	**28,772**	**26,672**

One variable is the complexity of your cut. If you have a lot of cuts and short pieces of film, that will increase either the cost of negative cutting or the number of hours required for an on-line. Other variables are the consistency of exposure on your camera negative *and* the quality of your original video transfer, which will affect the amount of time needed for color correction. As with mixing costs, there is more demand for transfer from film to digital video than existing facilities can readily handle. When there are no off hours, getting a discount can be pretty difficult.

Main & End Titles

The amount allowed for Titles would permit superimposing over scenes in *Desire Under the Magnolias*. Letters on black, a common choice for micro-budget shows, would be considerably less. Video titles, superimposed or on black, would be the cheapest of all in terms of cost *and* appearance.

5400	**Main & End Titles**							
5401	Main and End Titles		Allow			5,000	5,000	5,000
5411	Foreign Textless Version							0
						Total for 5400		5,000

Acct #	Description	Amount	Units	X	Rate	Subtotal	Total
5900	**Fringe Benefits**						
5999	Fringes						
	FICA	6.20	%		5,400	335	
	SUI/FUI	6.20	%		5,400	335	
	Medicare	1.45	%		5,400	78	
	Payroll Charges	0.25	%		5,400	14	
	Sales Tax	8.25	%		17,160	1,416	
	Clerical Comp	0.79	%		5,400	43	2,221
						Total for 5900	2,221
	TOTAL EDITING PERIOD						59,781

Fringe Benefits

These fringes are for the editorial staff only, and the Workmen's Comp rate on them is slightly lower than it is for production. Some producers treat them as clerical employees and pay at the lowest rate. If an editor is working a D-Vision system at a desk, the environment and risk factors would seem to justify this. If that D-Vision is in the editor's home and he or she is setting his or her (it's times like these when you really feel the need for a unisex pronoun) own hours, you might even legitimately qualify for an Independent Contractor arrangement and save the employee fringes.

6500	**Publicity**						
6501	Publicity Firm Fee						0
6502	Unit Publicist						0
6503	Neg., Prints, Supplies		Allow		750	750	750
6504	Prod. Publicity Costs						0
6585	Other Charges						0
					Total for 6500		750
6700	**Insurance**						
6701	Cast Insurance Package	325,000			0.05	16,250	16,250
6702	Negative Insurance						0
6703	Errors and Omissions						0
6704	Faulty Raw Stock & Camera						0
6705	Liability						0
6706	Workmen's Compensation						0
6707	Local Insurance Req.						0
6708	Misc. Equipment						0
6709	Comprehensive Liability						0
6710	Property Damage Liability						0
6785	Other Charges						0
					Total for 6700		16,250

Publicity

The cost of the Still Photographer's film and printing is the only item entered under Publicity.

Insurance

Insurance is the last thorny issue. A full insurance package breaks down into several sub-categories: (1) Negative and faulty stock, covering lab error, bad film or sound tapes, and, if you stretch it, scratches caused by human or mechanical malfunction; (2) Cast insurance against death or incapacity (normal is five leads and the director); (3) General Liability, against accidents with non-combatants; (4) Property, covering all rented equipment; (5) Workmen's Compensation; and (6) Errors and Omissions. Prices have increased in the past year. While they can still vary depending on policy limits, value of the items covered, and deductibles, the norm is now between 2% and 3.5% of the total budget. And, of course, micro-budgeteers are likelier to encounter minimum premiums that make the effective percentage even higher.

Insurance is a necessary evil, given that SAG, equipment-rental houses, municipalities where you shoot, and many people who rent locations will all require proof of coverage. Even if you try to shoot without insurance, it will be hard to shoot without Liability, Workmen's Comp., etc. What you do not have to buy are coverages 1, 2, or 6 above. We discuss the risk factors in *Hollywood on $5,000, $10,000, or $25,000 a Day.*

Acct #	Description	Amount	Units	X	Rate	Subtotal	Total
6800	**General Overhead**						
6801	Corporate Expense						0
6811	Office Rentals						
			Allow		1,000	1,000	1,000
6821	Furniture/Equip. Rentals						0
6835	Office Supplies		Allow		500	500	500
6841	Telephone and Telegraph		Allow		1,000	1,000	1,000
6851	Printing and Copying		Allow		750	750	750
6855	Postage and Delivery		Allow		250	250	250
6861	Entertainment						0
6871	Additional Allowances						0
6875	Production Service Org.						0
6885	Other Charges						0
						Total for 6800	3,500
7500	**Fees, Charges, & Misc.**						
7501	Legal Fee		Allow		3,500	3,500	3,500
7511	Tax Accounting						0
7531	MPAA Rating Fee						0
7541	Dialogue Continuity						0
7585	Other Charges						0
						Total for 7500	3,500
7900	**Fringe Benefits**						
7999	Fringes						
	Sales Tax	8.25	%		750	62	62
						Total for 7900	62

General Overhead

This is it, the last page of the budget (and again we've squeezed three accounts onto it). We should note here that, unlike pre-printed forms, you adjust the configuration of computer budgets. We told you earlier that the empty lines are important; and that is certainly true when you're filling out the budget. But we're also in favor of saving a tree or two, and that's the amount of paper it seems many shows use up. We're not telling you to print your budgets on the back of old scripts, though that's not a bad idea. Since the process of reviewing the empty lines takes place on the computer screen as you prepare the budget, after you've done a few, you may opt for the print setting that omits the empty accounts and saves a couple of pages. It is also not required to print each account on its own page, as we have mostly done here for purposes of illustrative clarity.

The amounts we're allowing for Office, Telephone etc. won't buy much; but many micro-budgeteers work out of their homes or scrounge some other facilities. We don't recommend this on anything approaching a normal budget (i.e., over $750,000), but it's not a bad idea when every dollar you save means that you can shoot another couple of feet of film. Printing and copying add up very fast, starting with the casting period if you're sending out scripts to a lot of actors. so, remember, save a tree. Since this is a "production" budget, there are several "delivery" items here such as the fee for an MPAA Rating ($2,000) and a Dialogue Continuity (around $1,000) that we're not including. If you plan on selling your micro-budget feature, be aware that these items, along with various picture and sound masters and perhaps isolated music and effects tracks and textless titles for foreign sales, will all be on the list of deliverables that most distributors will require.

Fees, Charges, & Misc.

Normal Legal Fees should be around 1% of the total budget; but on a micro-project that's not a lot. If you've got some good boiler-plate contracts and deal memos (hmmm, maybe that should be our next book), you can do these shows without a lawyer. But whatever forms you use, some lawyer somewhere should have glanced at them recently. Where do you find a lawyer? Well, you can look in the Yellow Pages or, better yet, you can ask around (preferably other micro-budget moviemakers) for a recommendation.

Whatever you do, remember that in a real sense, legal transcends the entire budget. It reaches back before production into fund raising and forward into distribution and profit participation. It is, sad to say, lurking behind every sandbag and prop tree, waiting to spring out and make your life miserable.

Fringe Benefits

What still more fringes? Actually, micro-budgeteers seldom have employees in these last few accounts, so no fringes are budgeted here. No cost—that's a lot more upbeat note than "make your life miserable" on which to end Part One.

Part Two

THE MICRO-
BUDGETEERS

Real Stories of the Micro Patrol

W e went out and talked to bunch of filmmakers about their micro-budget moviemaking experiences. We won't pretend that any of them seemed particularly thrilled to have worked, or still be working, with such limited resources—we edited out all of the actual moaning and groaning and tried to distill the essence.

These people agreed on a lot, but also had remarkable dissimilarities in approach. Although they both started out with the micro-budgeteer whose name middle-America is likeliest to recognize, Roger Corman, it would be hard to find more disparate attitudes than those of Larry Rattner and Jim Wynorski; and it would be hard to find a better prototype for micro-budget maven than Pirromount's founder. And while some of our interviewees never wanted to test the micro-budget waters again, all of them professed to have learned a lot from the experience, and those lessons are what we tried to get on tape.

If you bother to read the credits at the end of each section, you'll discover that a lot of these people have worked together. That's because it's a small micro-budget world after all. We wanted to talk mostly with producers and directors, many of whom, as you might have guessed, are also writers by default, but we also wanted to talk to some other people who are critical to the process: a director of photography, a composer, an editor, and a production manager. Finally, we wanted to talk exclusively with people whom we did not already know; we especially did not want to sit around and wax nostalgic about this or that catastrophe with a director of photography or production manager who had been shoulder-to-shoulder with us in the micro-budget trenches. So after tracking down and interviewing several producer types, we then spoke with a composer recommended by one of them, a director of photography suggested by a second, and a production manager mentioned by a third. We tried not to editorialize or make snide remarks during our chats, but, hey, some things are just stronger than we are.

We were gratified to discover that most of our fellow micro-budgeteers shared our frustrations and our enthusiasms. Maybe we'll start a club. If we do, and we ever want to take in new people, we'd better not make Jim Wynorski a charter member. (We really thought Wynorski was a hoot, as are his movies.) And we didn't put him last because of his advice to would-be competitors. After much discussion, a coin flip, and a best two-out-of-three in arm wrestling, the rational half of our writing team (no, we won't say who that is) prevailed, and we decided to present our interviewees in alphabetical order.

Interview *with* CHUCK CIRINO, Composer

CHUCK CIRINO is a musician who radiates enthusiasm for his work, no matter the level of the project, from *Chopping Mall* to *Munchie Strikes Back*. These titles don't have that big-budget ring to them, which means Cirino scores them by being, literally, a one-man band. We interviewed him surrounded by synthesizers, computers, tape recorders, video-editing equipment, etc., etc., all crammed into a small space. Music can make or break a movie, and Cirino knows the ins and outs of putting together a good score for peanuts.

Tell us how you got involved in film composing.

Through Jim Wynorski. I met him twenty years ago on my first honeymoon. We were both Ennio Morricone collectors, and we both had moved out to California. I was working as a video-tape editor, and Jim was working in advertising. Then Jim began working at Roger Corman's company, and Roger gave him a shot at directing *Killbots (Chopping Mall)*.

By this time, I had made a hobby of synthesizers, and Jim would come to me before I ever scored a film for him and say, "Let's do a cue just for the heck of it." So we'd watch an old Ennio Morricone film or we'd see *The Snow Devils* or *Omega Man*, and I'd do arrangements of the cues on the synthesizer just so that we'd have copies of these pieces of music.

At this point, I was directing Fred Rated commercials [for Federated Electronics] for Shadoe Stevens [DJ and actor]. We did over a thousand spots.

Would you consider these commercials micro-budget?

Ultra low-budget. We would shoot eight commercials in a day. I was the cameraman and the director.

How did you move from shooting commercials to scoring films?

Shadoe had put together a studio that included multi-track machines and synthesizers for his radio stuff. Jim knew I had access to this equipment, so he asked me, "Do you want to do the score for *Killbots?*"

Then on *Deathstalker II,* Jim had no money for sound—like two thousand dollars. He had to shoot it, edit it, and put it to-

gether somewhere down in South America. So before he left, I wrote fifteen minutes of music for him. Having access to Shadoe Stevens' equipment allowed me to score the film on a budget that I couldn't have done it for otherwise. Then, after a few years, I put together this studio that you're in. Before that, I had nothing.

I suggest that anybody who's getting into film should try to buy the equipment themselves if they don't already have it, or find somebody who's got a studio with synthesizers and work out a deal to use the equipment. That's the only way you're going to break in today.

What presents the most problems when you're scoring a low-budget film?

Time and budget. Time is always a problem. The budgets are always low.

What is the lowest sound-budget that you've worked with?

Twenty-five hundred dollars. Well, actually two thousand dollars for *Deathstalker II*. In that case, I created a music library for Jim Wynorski—I made him a bunch of cues that he liked—and a music editor cut it into the film. I wasn't really scoring to picture. We agreed on a love theme, I did several versions of it, and I did some stingers without even seeing the script.

What's the highest sound-budget that you've worked with?

Eighteen thousand. That was *The Return of Swamp Thing.*

Is there an astronomical difference between working in those two budget ranges?

Deathstalker II is the only film that I scored like that. So let's not use it. Let's use a Fred Olen Ray film, *The Alien Within*, which was a three-thousand-dollar budget. In that case, there was a big difference. On *Alien Within*, Fred left me alone. He knew that he had no money. He said, "Just go do it." Then he came in, did the approvals, and made a few changes. During *The Return of Swamp Thing*, Jim was over my shoulder every two days—the director-composer relationship kind of thing.

Do you think that you have more creative freedom when you have less money?

Yes, when you can call your own shots. Now, when I do anything under eight thousand dollars, I basically say, "Please leave me alone."

There's another aspect to this low-budget work that's very important and most people overlook completely—holding on to the copyright or publishing rights of the music. In a low-budget film, if you don't have a way of making money up front, you can get your money by keeping the copyright and the publishing. If you keep the copyright ownership of the music, then, when the music is aired on cable, you can make residuals through BMI or ASCAP.

Have you had any of your scores put on CD or tape?

No. I haven't had any record labels interested.

Why is that? Is it because low-budget film scores are not of interest to the public?

I think synthesizer scores just aren't popular, unless you're somebody like Hans Zimmer. He has money to work with when he does a score. He can go into a studio. That's the big difference. These guys are not doing them at home. They'll sequence them at home. They'll program them at home. But then they take their gear into a studio, and maybe bring real players in to enhance it. I don't have the time or the money to do that.

I have my equipment at home in my garage, I have no overhead except for electricity and maybe a new piece of equipment that I'll buy here and there. On a low-budget film, I do everything right in here. The biggest challenge has been being an engineer as well as a composer. You have to try to get the best sounds possible. I think that I don't get a lot of my stuff out on CDs because I don't hire an engineer—I am following the musical score through from conception to mastering to delivery. I do all the music editing myself, too, which is another good way to save money. Usually a composer—John Williams, Jerry Goldsmith, etc.—works from the cue sheets given to him by a music editor. I don't bother with that. I don't have time for that. I basically put the tape of the film in, spot it with the director, and write a few notes down.

Right now I'm doing *Temptress* for Jim Wynorski. There are no notes. Basically he says, "Chuck, you know what to do here." We have a real neat shorthand going between us right now that works ninety percent of the time. Sometimes I'll miss something, and he'll come in and say, "You missed this," or "No, I had this in mind here." But that again depends on the budget. If it's a low budget, leave me alone. On *Dinosaur Island,* Fred Ray and Jim Wynorski had no money. They had like thirty-five hundred dollars. It was the first independent film that they did on their own, and at the time they couldn't afford me because I'd worked my budgets up. But I said, "I wanna do this film for fun. Just let me have the publishing and let me do whatever I want." They left me completely alone. Then they made a couple of little changes. I always allow the director to make a few changes. Whether I have complete autonomy or not, I still let the director come and listen to it before we lay it down because nobody likes surprises on the dub stage.

Could you describe what the process is after a producer or director approaches you and says, "I want a score for my film"?

It's almost always slightly different. Let's say you go to a new film company where you're probably up against two or three other guys. You will be invited to a screening of the film, and usually there will be another one or two composers there. You'll sit down, watch the film, and you'll go home. Or maybe you won't go home; maybe the producer will take you off to the side, one composer at a time, and ask you how you like the film. I don't know how a producer chooses a composer in this case. I think he chooses a composer based on how much the composer liked the film or how much he thought he could do for it. At that time, they may ask you to do a demo. They'll listen to your demo; they'll give you a scene and then they'll listen to the cues you've done for the scene. Sometimes they'll ask you to do another demo, or they will ask you to change the style, which I've done before.

Now that can be a problem because I write in a certain style. When a company came to me lately and asked, "Can you do a score in this other style?" I did a demo and the demo sounded great. Then they said, "Score the whole film that way." Well, I was completely out of my realm. That can become a problem.

After they hire you, then you go through your contractual hoops, as I call them. Most of the time the contract doesn't get completed until after the film is done, but I suggest that you get the contract done beforehand as much as possible. However, you, as the composer, always have the upper hand until the contract is signed because they can't legally put your music in the film until you sign the contract.

At the contract stage, you will be bickering about publishing, about delivery dates, about money. The lower the money, the more leverage you have unless you are up against other guys who will give up publishing rights or do it cheaper. Until recently, producers didn't know what publishing rights were. Now they all know.

After the contract is done, you'll sit down with the director or the producer or both and you'll spot the film. If you don't have a music editor, you do all the spotting yourself. You'll write down in-points and out-points for each cue. You'll make some notes on where the director wants stingers. You're best off, I believe, taking these notes before you start the score. Then you'll go over the film with your notes, find out how much music you need altogether, find out where you can use a theme over and over. In my films, the scores are very, very thematic. Jim likes that. Fred likes that. And I've found out that most producers and directors like thematic scores. Then, when you are done with the initial cue sheets, you'll start scoring the film.

In the past, I have ignored the main titles until I've completely scored the film. You should do those last because you never know when you're going to come up with a wonderful theme. You may write a theme up front and then find out that you've written a better theme later on.

So you go ahead and score the film. And I've done this differently each time. Sometimes, if you're in a time-bind, you mix as you go. And that's what I'm doing now with my new film, *The Temptress*. I'm mixing my final mix as I write each cue. Sometimes you'll have the luxury of writing the entire score and then be able to go back and mix each cue in a two-day mix session. If you have the time and the money for that, that's fine. I usually do it as I go.

When you're done with all the cues, you have to lay them into the picture. I used to take the cues, one by one, to the dub stage and lay them in wild, which took six or seven hours. Now there's new digital-editing technology that allows you to do your music editing at home, which is what I do here. I take my equipment with me to the dub stage, sync it up via SMPTE [video time code], and lay all the music in one pass [the length of the film].

Producers and directors love you if you can do this because you've only used up two hours of studio time as opposed to seven hours. A composer who's just getting in is a hero if he can save the producer money on the dub stage. I suggest that composers do that. Even if they have to use their money to rent this equipment, or borrow it, the producer will love them for it later on.

Once it's in, you walk away from the picture and hopefully you get paid. I only once had a payment problem.

What do you think is the ideal relationship between a composer and a director or producer?

Well, Jim and I have an ideal relationship. It's ideal because we have the same musical tastes. We listen to music from the same movies.

When you're working with a new director, the best way to speak to him is in terms of other scores that you have done or that he likes. That's how you get a good relationship going. I suggest that young composers wanting to get into film take directing classes and meet young directors because those directors have not chosen their composer yet. When they're doing their student films, the composer can jump in and score them. They can then start a rapport early on in each of their careers. That's a good way to go.

Is the competition fierce among composers?

Absolutely. When I first got into it, there were very few synthesizer composers who I can think of. But since then, anyone who's ever been in a rock band is now a film composer. I mean, everyone who's got MIDI gear calls himself a composer. Once you do one film, you're a film composer.

Is there any film that you worked on that you thought had insurmountable problems?

Yes. But I won't mention the film. I was asked to do a second demo that wasn't within my style. I was scared because the money was decent and they were asking me to do something that was out of my realm. The problem wasn't just musical, it was political. There were people who put their reputations on the line for me to get this job. I didn't know the director. The producers came in and said, "We want you." The director said, "I want somebody else." So I had to please someone who already didn't like me. Two weeks into the score, we got hit with the earthquake. All of my equipment came down on the floor, and I had a week to put it back together again. Then they weren't honest about the deadlines—they told me that I had a deadline, and, when I met the deadline and I delivered the score, which they approved, they wanted me to start making changes. Well, I had already started another film. That's when we got into a major conflict.

Was the budget low on this one?

No. It wasn't as high as *The Return of Swamp Thing*, but it was decent. And it still wasn't enough money to get it done correctly. I went out-of-pocket and brought players in.

It was a hexed project. Because I didn't have time to do the changes, they rescored it with another composer, which led me to believe that all the deadlines they gave me were total fabrications. It was a very hurtful experience. I suggest that you find somebody who's going to be truthful to you about deadlines.

Is there a great difference between scoring a comedy and scoring a drama?

Oh, yeah. I really love comedy. With comedy you can go wild. You can mimic classical music and other composers. You can do soundalikes for comedy's sake.

I scored a TV series that I directed, *Amazing Live Sea Monkeys*, which aired on Saturday mornings a few years ago. This was one of best experiences of my life. The Chiodo Brothers, who made the film *Killer Klowns from Outer Space,* got a TV series on CBS. They liked me as a director, so they called me in and I directed two episodes. Then, when it was time to do the score, they didn't know what they were doing or who to call. They were looking at some composers whom I had never heard of. I had to question whether the composers they were looking at could pull it off or not, but I didn't say anything. Well, apparently the other composers fell through. At the very last minute, they said, "Chuck, can you compose it? Can you do comedy?" "Yeah, I just did *Munchie* and I've done a couple of other comedies." It turned out to be a very wonderful experience. My scores were for the episodes that I directed.

Now there are two ways to score a comedic scene. One way is with wacky, silly, zany music. The other way is to score a comedic scene with completely serious music. I prefer the latter. There's a cue I did for a really funny scene in *Munchie Strikes Back* that is very dark, mock Edgar Allan Poe. I scored it with a very serious piece of music, which made it all the funnier.

Drama is more difficult. You have to take more time with it. You can't go over the top too much. You've got to pull back on the music.

Are you interested in pursuing your career as a director?

Yeah, yeah. Jim has offered me films, five-day wonders.

Would you give up composing?

No, I want to do both. I'm actually developing some TV series of my own. I'm really into the guerrilla-video syndrome, down and dirty, reality-TV stuff.

Do you think the information network with its supposed five hundred channels will open up the market for those kinds of films or videos?

Absolutely. I want my own channel. I don't mean that literally. I want my own two-hour block on a satellite station. You're still going to have networks, but then you're also going to have all these producers and directors who have their own equipment, and they're going to be doing their own programs, specialty shows, camping shows, cooking shows. And I think they are going to be incredibly interesting. You may not be able to watch a whole half-hour, but as these people get better at what they do, I think you are going to see some fascinating stuff. The government will no longer be able to control what you see. That's what I like about it. Before music I was doing public-access TV. My first job was in public-access television and I did a couple of my own TV series. Young filmmakers will have a venue now. And they'll be able to make a little bit of money because they'll be able to sell commercials on their own little TV show.

What advice would you give young filmmakers or composers coming into the business now? What do they need to survive?

One of two things: get another job that allows them a lot of time to do what they want to do on weekends and at night and that pays enough money that they can go out and buy some gear. Or they need a wife or husband who's pulling it all together for them and believes in them enough to let them do what they're doing while the other one works.

Credits (as Composer)

Chopping Mall (1986). Director: Jim Wynorski. Cast: Paul Bartel, Mary Woronov.

Deathstalker II (1986). Director: Jim Wynorski. Cast: John Terlesky, Monique Gabrielle.

Big Bad Mama II (1987). Director: Jim Wynorski. Cast: Angie Dickinson, Robert Culp.

Terror Squad (1987). Director: Peter Maris. Cast: Chuck Connors, Kerry Brennan.

Not of This Earth (1988). Director: Jim Wynorski. Cast: Traci Lords, Arthur Roberts.

Deadly Stranger (1988). Director: Max Kleven. Cast: Darlanne Fluegel, Michael J. Moore.

Transylvania Twist (1988). Director: Jim Wynorski. Cast: Teri Copley, Howard Morris, Robert Vaughn.

Beverly Hills Vamp (1988). Director: Fred Olen Ray. Cast: Eddie Deezen, Britt Ekland.

The Return of Swamp Thing (1989). Director: Jim Wynorski. Cast: Heather Locklear, Louis Jordan, Sarah Douglas.

Alienator (1989). Director: Fred Olen Ray. Cast: Jan-Michael Vincent, John Phillip Law, P.J. Soles.

A Man Called Sarge (1990). Director: Stuart Gillard. Cast: Gary Kroeger, Marc Singer.

Mob Boss (1990). Director: Fred Olen Ray. Cast: Morgan Fairchild, Eddie Deezen.

Soldier's Fortune (1990). Director: Arthur N. Mele. Cast: Gil Gerard, Dan Haggerty.

The Haunting of Morella (1990). Director: Jim Wynorski. Cast: Nicole Eggert, David McCallum.

Evil Toons (1990). Director: Fred Olen Ray. Cast: David Carradine, Madison Stone, Artc Johnson.

Sorority House Massacre II (1990). Director: Jim Wynorski. Cast: Robyn Harris, Melissa Moore.

Haunting Fear (1991). Director: Fred Olen Ray. Cast: Delia Sheppard, Jan-Michael Vincent, Karen Black.

976-Evil II (1991). Director: Jim Wynorski. Cast: Brigitte Nielsen, Rene Assa.

The Alien Within (1991). Director: Fred Olen Ray.

Munchie (1991). Director: Jim Wynorski. Cast: Loni Anderson, Andrew Stevens.

Inner Sanctum (1991). Director: Fred Olen Ray. Cast: Tanya Roberts, Joseph Bottoms, Margaux Hemingway.

Hard To Die (1991). Director: Jim Wynorski. Cast: Robyn Harris.

Angel Eyes (1992). Director: Fred Olen Ray. Cast: Monique Gabrielle.

Sins of Desire (1992). Director: Jim Wynorski. Cast: Tanya Roberts, Jan-Michael Vincent, Delia Sheppard.

Body Chemistry III (1993). Director: Jim Wynorski. Cast: Andrew Stevens, Morgan Fairchild.

Dinosaur Island (1993). Directors: Fred Olen Ray, Jim Wynorski.

Ghoulies 4 (1993). Director: Jim Wynorski.

Munchie Strikes Back (1993). Director: Jim Wynorski.

Inner Sanctum II (1993). Director: Fred Olen Ray. Cast: David Warner, Margaux Hemingway.

Possessed by the Night (1994). Director: Fred Olen Ray. Cast: Shannon Tweed.

Interview *with* TIM EVERITT, Writer/Director et al.

TIM EVERITT is a filmmaker who doesn't like "delegating the filmmaking." Consequently, he produces, writes, directs, shoots, and edits his films. He's probably been tempted to act and record sound, too, but we didn't get into that. Perhaps that would mean the actors would outnumber the crew, which is never a good concept. Everitt had family connections *and* he went to film school. Since graduating, he's paid the rent by doing commercials, but features are his first love, and he's trying to get each successive budget to increase exponentially.

How did you get involved in low-budget filmmaking?

I went to USC, and they train you to make low-budget features.

USC trains you to make low-budget features? News to us. So you made some student films there?

Yes.

After you got out of USC, how did you make your first non-student film?

A friend of mine and I raised independent financing. It was very micro-budget. It was called *Furious*.

When was that made?

1985. My whole story is that my father was in television—he owned TV stations. So I shot films from the time I was a little boy. And all I ever did in high school and pretty much in college was shoot industrials. By the time I got out of USC, I had a professional demo reel that I'd been working on for ten years. That's how I got into commercials immediately after film school, and how I started breaking into the feature business, which is hard to do.

So, after doing these commercials for a couple of years, you approached a millionaire acquaintance to finance a feature?

That's correct.

Did you have a script?

No, we did not. We just convinced him that it would be a good idea to back our film project.

Neat trick. Did you have a budget in mind?

Yes. We had a thirty-thousand-dollar budget for the completed 35mm picture.

Did that include salaries for anyone or was that just the material costs?

We paid the actors. And we actually had a few thousand left over, which we kept in our pocket. The actual cash cost was nineteen thousand, and we bought about eight-thousand-dollars worth of equipment—a synchronizer, a Nagra, stuff like that.

How many feet did you shoot?

Under a two-to-one ratio. I cut the flash frames [overexposed frames usually at the beginning and ends of rolls of film] out and put the movie together. We even had a sequence in which we used the flash frames—an hallucination in which the main character flashed back on all these things that had happened. It was hard to do on thirty thousand dollars.

Did you go to a low-budget lab?

No. Part of our plan was to save cost on the answer print. We wanted to make a special deal, just one pass and we'd take the first print. Our concept was to get the very finest processing so that the negative was flawless. So we went to the MGM lab. Back then, they and the Deluxe lab were the two finest in town. We negotiated a really good deal. We were shooting such little film that they put us on a sort of commercial/experimental-film budget rate instead of their feature rate. We got a good deal on

the sound mix, too, which we mixed at Glen Glenn, the top place in town.

You mixed at Glen Glenn, too? Did you spend money on anything else?

Just gas and lunch. We gave the actors like a hundred dollars a day.

How many days did you shoot?

We shot seven days.

We assume these were non-SAG actors.

They were non-SAG actors. They were awful. It was like a martial-arts movie, so we cast them based on their karate skills more than on their acting skills.

What about the locations?

We filmed on the west side and places we could get for free. We didn't bother with any permits or police.

Did you have any chase scenes?

Yes, we had some big ones.

You just jumped in the car and did them?

Yeah, we did all these marginally illegal things. We even had some scenes where we landed a helicopter in a state park.

Were there a lot of people on the crew?

No, two of us. There were only twelve or thirteen lines of dialogue in the movie.

Two people! Did you buy any other equipment?

We bought a moviola that belonged to Robert Flaherty [for those who don't know, a documentary moviemaker of some repute] that had belts. And it really, really worked.

When you had the finished answer print, did you have a plan for the film?

The plan was to show it around to distributors, try to get it picked up.

Did you get it picked up?

We got it picked up by Atlantic Pictures. At that time, they had just finished *Valley Girl* and some other big pictures.

Did you get any money back on the picture?

We didn't get any money in advance on the picture, but they did sell some territories. And we did recoup our costs and then some.

Now the second picture, *The Runaway,* was that done soon after *Furious*?

No, much later, in 1988.

Why did you wait so long?

Because I was busy. I had started my own production company and we were doing a lot of commercial work and syndicated TV work. And I had used my only millionaire for *Furious*.

So this wasn't a different millionaire?

No, I put up my own money for *The Runaway.*

Assuming that you had made your money back on the first picture, why did your original millionaire not want to go again?

We didn't make that much money. He was in hotels and he was a busy guy.

And was *The Runaway* SAG or non-SAG?

Non-SAG. This was like an actors' workshop movie. It was based on the idea that we'll put a whole big cast together out of somebody's workshop because these people have that "Hey, kids, let's put on a play" attitude. And we'll see if we can make a decent picture.

Did you write the script on that premise?

Yes.

I imagine that, in order to get a demo reel, these actors donated their time?

Actually, we paid the leads because we shot for two weeks. It's hard to take time off; we wanted to compensate them somehow.

That was somewhat generous, assuming that your budget was in the same area.

It was even lower. It was fourteen thousand. And that was for 35mm. We used a line of credit to pay for production costs. It was all done on credit—cameras, lab . . . by this time we had established pretty good credit. We got one hundred and twenty days on our credit at CFI [film lab].

So the plan was to sell it and have, if not the money, at least a deal?

Yeah, get the deal and try to pay off the creditors.

Did that work?

Not quite. It took a little while for us to get the money back. We just made payments and extended the payments until we got the money back.

This was 1988. Did you follow the same process for selling this as you did for the other film?

We ended up with a salesman who was handling international for Shapiro/Glickenhaus. He handled the movie and sold the foreign.

Did you sell domestic on either of these films?

I didn't sell domestic on *Runaway,* but I did on *Furious.* It actually is still in video stores in certain parts of town if you dig for it.

What video company put it out?

VC II.

Was that a sale that Atlantic arranged?

No, we arranged it.

Did you repeat the first experience and make a profit?

Yes, we did.

And you immediately took that profit and made a third picture?

No, we waited a few years and continued making commercials until just last year when we made our third picture [*Fatally Yours*].

I assume this was a higher budget and the financing was put together in a different way?

We had a guy who wanted to get into the movie business, and we had experience making ultra low-budget movies.

So this was twenty times the budget of your previous films?

Three hundred and fifty thousand dollars.

Did you budget it that way when you approached him or did it come out of his willingness to spend more money?

His original idea was to spend about sixty thousand. And we said, "Sure, okay." As the project developed, we kept telling him what money we needed for what we wanted to do, and it just escalated until he was in for about three hundred and fifty thousand before he started saying "no." We kept wondering when he was going to start saying "no."

It sounds so easy. You just open the spigot and the money comes out.

Well, eventually he said "no." He got a little overextended, but the picture turned out good. We like it a lot.

Did the budget increase incrementally as you went along?

Yes.

Was part of it because of cast?

Yes. He [the investor] originally wanted to do it non-SAG. Then we lined up some SAG actors who were going to come in non-SAG, but the union got word of it. So if we were to keep our key players, like Roddy McDowall, we would have to go SAG, and there goes the budget.

You also had to post a bond, I assume?

Yes, we did. You post, I think, a third of what you're going to pay them.

Did these deals with actors also involve participation or was it just salary and that was the end of it?

The big stars have a deferment. They were paid in cash, minimum, plus a deferment after the picture gets sold.

After the deferments are paid, your company has all the profits?

That's correct.

How did you acquire your name cast?

Through the millionaire's girlfriend, a girl named Ingrid Boulting who, I think, was Ingrid Superstar from the sixties. She was a big model, and she was one of the superstars of Andy Warhol's factory. She knew all these strange people, and she talked them into being in the movie.

Before, you were "marginally illegal." Were you now fully permitted and insured?

Yes, all the permits, all the insurance, everything.

On the previous show, *The Runaway*, did you have any insurance?

Well, by the time I made *The Runaway*, I had my own production company. As a production company, we carry a million dollars liability, standard insurances. So we just ran everything through the company.

What about *Furious*?

We didn't have insurance. It was by the seat of our pants.

Well, that's the way a lot of people who are reading this book are going to make films.

It's okay. You can do it that way. But if something goes wrong, if someone falls off a ladder, you're dead. The first film was me and another guy and an Arri II. We didn't even rent anything on that film. There were zero rentals.

Have you got distribution on the most recent picture?

The millionaire guy who wants to break into Hollywood is doing the sales.

When did you actually finish it?

In February of 1994.

Did you shoot and edit *Fatally Yours* yourself as you did the other films?

That's correct.

Is that better for you than working with a director of photography?

I guess so. I just make the film. If you're a filmmaker, you just get in there and make the film as opposed to delegating the filmmaking to a lot of other people. I like to shoot—I operate the camera. I can see the framing. I know if it's right. I can see if we hit the focus marks.

Do you plan to continue to work on this level? Are you happy working on micro-budget shows?

Currently, we are planning to do a few pictures that are at this two-hundred-and-fifty to three-hundred-thousand-dollar range. We've got some deals from some people. And we're going to be starting production on some movies in the next month or two. We would like to work on higher levels because three hundred and fifty thousand dollars is not enough to make a really good movie. Seriously, folks, you need more money than that.

Do you have any final advice for filmmakers coming in at this level?

If you want to continue working, you should pay your suppliers and be very honest with people. Don't burn people. Because we're in Hollywood, we have access to great pools of talent. It's a good idea to be SAG because you can tap that talent pool. That's a huge advantage. If you're in Dallas or somewhere, then it's not so important. You try to get people you can really, really work with.

We've gotten better as filmmakers over the years. And hopefully we'll get better still. It takes skill and practice.

Credits (as Producer/Director/Writer/ Cinematographer/Editor)

Furious (1985).

The Runaway (1988). Cast: Gracie Moore.

Fatally Yours (1994). Cast: Rick Rossovich, Roddy McDowall, George Lazenby.

Interview *with* PETER JENSEN, Cinematographer

PETER JENSEN is a cinematographer/filmmaker who found that life after film school ranged from shooting documentaries about Bengal tigers to working as a camera assistant on *Fantasy Island*. Over the last decade, he has built up a formidable résumé doing Steadicam work for filmmakers as disparate as Francis Ford Coppola and Aaron Spelling. But, besides these higher-end productions, he still puts plenty of time in at the micro- and low-budget salt mines, sometimes acting as both director/writer and cinematographer. When we spoke to him, he was preparing to shoot a promo for his own script, a formula he successfully applied with *Grandmother's House*. He is called "Doc" by his colleagues for his professorial manners and sage advice.

How did you get started in films?

When I was about ten years old, some family friends of ours, the Schickeles, in Fargo, North Dakota, where I grew up, were filmmakers. At that time, they were in high school. Now, one of them, Peter, a.k.a. P.D.Q. Bach, is a composer and the other, David, is a film producer working up in San Francisco. They were really remarkable kids. About 1954, we moved into the Schickele house when they moved out. That house had a little theater in the basement with curtains and costumes and a little projection booth, so we started making our own 8mm films. Then, when I was in high school, I got a job with a local company that was doing some fairly big-budget industrial films based on the farm economy. It was run by Bill Schneider, and was a tremendous help to me because I was able to use all their equipment. And, when I was in college, I would come home and work for them on summer projects.

I had one experience with Schneider Films that was probably the most important film experience of my entire career. I shot a scene from my student film—a twenty-five minute expression of my view of life, my philosophy—and, when I got the dailies developed at a local TV station, I was amazed to see that the camera, as I panned, would go off level. They were the most incredibly ugly dailies I'd ever seen in my life. They were a shock. The members of the film company were brutal in their criticism—they drank beer and they laughed. So I went out and did it again, and the dailies were still terrible. Actually, I reshot that scene about five or six times. By the sixth time, they looked pretty much like what I had conceived. I learned a lot. I learned to be hardened to criticism. I learned how to keep the camera level, how to keep it focused, and how to expose film correctly.

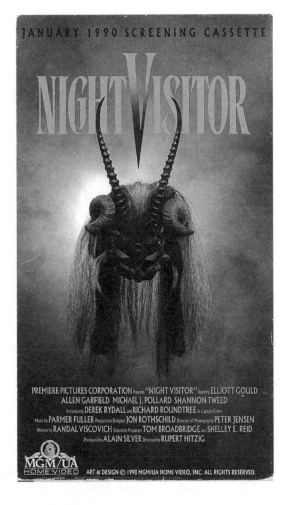

So what did you do after you did the industrial films?

I came to UCLA and started doing student films. I ultimately did my thesis film at UCLA. It was *No Deposit, No Return*.

Can you tell us a little bit about that film?

It was done in a way that I'd never do another film again. I started it without having a complete script. Back in 1968, when I was working on that film, there were lots of films that were improvised, so I thought that this is a possible way to make it. Writing a script, at that point, was beyond me. What we ended up with was a huge jumble of fairly mediocre footage that was very difficult to edit together.

Was it feature length?

Yes. It was.

What was the budget on it?

About one hundred thousand dollars.

And how did you get financing for it?

I was approached by two businessmen from Ohio. They had the very best intentions. I had the very best intentions. And the film did get some kind of distribution.

Theatrical?

Yes. The film has some very strong redeeming qualities about it. Originally, we had a cameraman and I was the director only. But we had some problems scheduling the cameraman because we couldn't pay him much money. It was just an impossible thing to work out, and ultimately, I ended up doing the camera work myself. I would prepare for about three or four days for a weekend of shooting. By the time Saturday morning came around, I was so exhausted and overwhelmed with all the work I'd been doing that when I arrived on the set I had trouble concentrating. I just couldn't focus. I had a tough time taking the camera out of the case because I was casting, directing, doing all the production work. I was a one-man band in the most literal sense.

Did you have any other crew members?

Very few, and they were very undependable. I learned that that kind of film production is tremendously exhausting, which was a very important lesson.

Do you think that the main problem on that film was no script or no crew?

No script. But also the way I was producing it—a little at a time—made it into a kind of student film that just got longer and longer.

How long was your shooting schedule?

It was shot over a period of nine months.

How many actual shooting days was that?

It probably averaged about a day or two every week. I was also taking classes at UCLA at that time.

The end result was a mixture of what I consider very good footage and what looked like a beginning student film. I learned so much on that project. It was shot 16mm on a reversal film stock 7252 and then blown up to 35mm. It was a startlingly good-looking blow-up.

I also learned some lessons about insurance on that film. We ran into some situations that were potentially dangerous. One of them was when we did group scenes for which we would recruit people from the Venice Beach boardwalk. They were the archetype hippies of the 1960s. The man who was helping me do the dialogue writing told me that there were some quintessential hippies whom he had met on the boardwalk. So I went to talk to them. They were bizarre looking and the women were very young, teenagers actually. They were going to be my extras. And, since I was also the transportation department, of course, I went to pick them up. Just as I was about to knock on their door, they came bursting out through it. Angel Jesus, the leader, was crying. That was very unusual because he was . . . macho wouldn't be the word . . . he was more satanic, which was one of the reasons why everyone wanted to get him in my film. My extras said that they were going out to the desert; they said something terrible was going to happen to them. So they drove off and disappeared. Well, two mornings later I opened up the *L.A. Times* and there were my extras on the front page, standing there with Charles Manson. It turned out that, little did I know, I was recruiting people from the Venice branch of the Manson Family. I was extremely lucky—just when I could have gotten into a lot of trouble, they were rounded up and arrested.

This is an archetypal example of getting into a lot of trouble by recruiting extras from the street, sweeping them up from questionable locations.

I also put extras at risk on that project when we transported a whole bunch of kids whom we had vacuumed right off the boardwalk into La Tuna Canyon to do a commune scene. We built tents and we had ropes attached to the sides of the cliff by nails. We transported the kids up in this old, rickety bus and told them that they should stay by it. The trip up there was bad enough because the bus barely made it, and for the first time in my life, it occurred to me that insurance was probably a good idea. And then, despite the fact that we were yelling and screaming at them, they scrambled up the sides of these hills. I was sure the ropes were going to come loose and that the kids were going to fall. Luckily, no one did, and we finally got the scene. When we left, we left with most of them; some of them had scrambled off into the distance. Today there would be hell to pay for doing something like that.

How did you get locations?

Very rarely did we pay for locations. We got permission from people to use their houses. I told people I was a filmmaker from UCLA, and that worked.

What did you work on after that?

There was nothing going on except very big pictures for union cameramen, which I was not, so I shot educational films and documentaries. Then I did what I think was the smartest thing in my career—I bought a camera in partnership with someone else. We bought an Eclair NPR, which is a very good investment. It made its money back many, many times. My partner actually shot several low-budget feature films in 16mm with the NPR and made quite a bit of money on them.

Do you see any difference in quality between shooting a film in 16mm and 35mm?

There's a big difference between 16 and 35. 35 has very definite advantages. A 35mm negative going to a one-inch video master has a certain kind of authority to it, a sharpness that a 16mm does not. 16mm has another quality to it—you can actually see the grain structure, and sometimes this can work for you. Actually, I think that going from 16mm negative to one-inch master is a very ethereal combination.

Were they doing that kind of transferring to tape in the '70s in low-budget?

No, not until the 1980s when video come into play in distribution.

I learned some lessons from telecine. I think it's important to control the process of going from negative to one-inch master. It will make more difference than almost any other single factor in the film. In many ways, it's more important than your release print, especially on a low-budget project, because video is the main way your film is going to be distributed. The telecine operator is crucial. You need someone who knows what he's doing.

How do you shoot a film, make a film look good, give the director what he or she wants, and still stay within the limits of time inherent in a low-budget film?

Necessity is often the mother of invention. Many great things have been done on low-budget films, and they have been done because there are certain parameters set ahead of time. I think that that's the key thing. I think you have to conceptualize within certain guidelines. If you have your concepts set ahead of time, you can do incredible things. You can light your foreground, you can light your actors and choose locations in which the background lights itself, for instance, neon or high light-level in the background. You can even choose a city to work in that is naturally illuminated, a city that is friendly to filmmaking. Many cities around the country will go out of their way to get a film shot there. They'll deploy their police department, their fire department, and give you permits for very little cost, including blocking off highways and supplying just about anything you need.

Often the look of a film comes from where it's being shot. You shoot a film on a huge budget, but if it's a bad location with bad art direction—if those elements are not working for you—you are going to have a hell of a time making a decent film. However, if you are working in a beautiful location, you can do something that looks far better. I had one such experience when I shot a film in Redlands, California, which is one of the most beautiful towns in the state. It's filled with Victorian houses, orange groves, underground passageways that were built by Indians back in the 1840s for irrigation. It is the most beautifully lyrical place I've ever seen anywhere in the United States. The sun hits the place just the right way. Even when there's smog in the San Bernardino Valley, where it's located, it seems beautiful—it seems to leave a beautiful haze. In fact, I found the place was so suggestive of stories, also of shots I could do, that I ultimately wrote a script and got about a million dollars to shoot it there.

This was which film?

Grandmother's House.

And you managed to raise the money on your own?

With my partner, yes.

Often that's the hardest element for a low- or micro-budget filmmaker. How do you get the money?

I think you have to be enthusiastic. You can actually talk an idea and get an idea sold.

You produced and shot *Grandmother's House*?

Yes. Compared to what I'd done before, we had a really large crew, and they were very hard-working, largely younger people. We knew Redlands very well by that time. And we knew a lot of people in Redlands. One of them was somehow connected with the radio station, and he lined up a lot of people in town as extras. To do this, we used many techniques that are used by major studios today—getting people to a large stadium by promising them prizes, etc., using radio stations, DJs, etc. to get people to come and provide background. You can get a lot of people for a small amount of money.

How did you acquire your actors?

We were limited to using non-SAG actors.

Do you think that's a mistake?

I think SAG is the best investment you can possibly make.

What about acquiring crew?

We were paying fairly small amounts of money.

How do you keep their enthusiasm up when you are paying small amounts of money? They can walk at any time.

Crews very rarely walk. They have a very high sense of professionalism. When people have walked, it's not been because of money. If it's agreed upon at the beginning, then they will usually follow through. There have been problems only when the producer or someone else is insensitive to their needs. When the season is busy, it's obviously hard to find crew members who are willing to work for small amounts of money. And, obviously, you don't have the budget to pay more. I personally believe that if you are going to hire people at the entry level, you need to keep an eye on them to make sure they are not doing things that are dangerous or foolish. If you are using stunt people, make sure you are using stunt people who are not just trying to get a reel at any cost. On many projects, I have seen stunt men who are not very established do stunts that they shouldn't do.

How many days did you shoot on the film?

Probably thirty, thirty-five days.

When you are shooting a film on the low-budget level, is there ever a time when you, the director of photography, say, "No, we can't do that shot within the limits of this film"?

Sure. If it is impossible, you have to say it. It's very important for the director of photography to draw the line as clearly as he can. Otherwise you can get involved in something that is a real black hole.

Wouldn't that be the case more often on a low-budget or micro-budget film because you don't have elaborate equipment or time, etc.?

Not necessarily. Often you can do very elaborate shots with very simple equipment. The key thing is time and intelligence in planning out the shot and the advance notice that you have before you do the shot. You can build things—steadicams, dollies, cranes, etc.—with a hammer and nails. You can do spectacular effects on a low-budget film. Actually, low-budget films have an advantage over larger-budgeted films because the larger films cost a huge amount of money and everyone is aware of how much money is going down the drain. On low-budget projects, time is cheap and oftentimes pre-production time is very cheap. You can build rigs and things. Your imagination is your limit. The nature of the budget doesn't necessarily correspond to how spectacular the shot is. It's all in planning ahead of time. When the shots are not planned out ahead of time, the director on the set is telling the cameraman, "Gee, I'd like to do this and this," but there's very little time to get the resources together, there's very little flexibility because of the time element. You're just stuck with what you've got.

What kind of distribution did you have on *Grandmother's House*?

It was sold through the American Film Market. Basically, it was designed for video distribution.

What do you think is the ideal relationship between the director and the cinematographer?

I think that you probably have to add another member there—the writer.

You are trying to realize a concept, and the director of photography really has to understand the concept, not only understand the letter of it but the spirit of it. The writer, the director, and the cinematographer have to work together. Unfortunately, a lot of films are made sort of accidentally. They're compromised. And filming is a series of compromises as it is.

On a lot of low-budget projects, you may actually end up with less compromise because you can take that pre-production time and use it the way you want to, and you can have more pre-production time if you want. The more pre-planning that is done, the better the result is going to be.

The problem with filmmaking on a larger scale is that you start with an idea, and then, by the time you start realizing the idea, it's in the hands of all these other people. It's like controlling a team of wild horses. What you end up with is ultimately something that is a lot different than what you conceived. On a low-budget, there is more chance of controlling the concept if you are the director-writer or writer-producer.

For instance, you can have the biggest crew in the world with all the lighting gear imaginable, and, if you are shooting a location where lighting is crucial, such as the desert, and you're not shooting at the right time of day, it's going to look the same whether you have a large crew or a small one, a big budget or a low budget. That's why in a low-budget situation, if you're shooting, for example, Ingmar Bergman-style, with a very small crew and you're waiting around for just the right sunlight, you can obviously come up with superior results. Results that are so good that they will surprise people who have been working in the business for a long time and who are forced to shoot a certain number of pages each day.

Over the last several years, you've concentrated on steadicam work for large-budget films? Do you plan to go back into low-budget some day?

I sure do. I like to shoot films in locations I love, like the desert. Personally, a film is not worth making unless I'm having some fun with the project. I really love to film in places where I feel comfortable and places that are exciting, and I love to work with people who are really enjoying what they are doing.

Do you have any advice for people coming into the low-budget field now?

The opportunity today is tremendous. There are many more people in the business today, but there are many more projects.

We are going to see a lot of productions starting off in a lot of new places around the country and the world. Take China for example. It's a major market, a major location. There's a real future in this.

Credits (as Cinematographer)

No Deposit, No Return (1972). Also Director and Producer. Cast: Melinda Marx.

Bengal Tiger (1972). Documentary. Producer: Richard Martin.

Ghosts of Cape Horn (1974). Documentary. Producer: Keith Critchlow.

California Reich (1977). Documentary. Directors: Walter Parkes, Keith Critchlow.

Kiss Daddy Goodbye (1982). Producer: Alain Silver. Director: Patrick Regan. Cast: Fabian Forte, Marilyn Burns.

Terror Squad (1987). Director: Peter Maris. Cast: Chuck Connors.

Grandmother's House (1988). Also Co-produced. Director: Peter Rader. Cast: Eric Foster, Brinke Stevens.

Night Visitor (1989). Producer: Alain Silver. Director: Rupert Hitzig. Cast: Elliott Gould, Allen Garfield.

Interview *with* ZANE LEVITT, Producer

ZANE LEVITT is a fast-talking, intelligent filmmaker who required little prompting to give us the information we wanted. His art-training background at the San Francisco Art Institute shows in the look of his productions. His micro-budget *Liquid Dreams* has a slick, music-video feel which belies its $300,000 budget. He has also co-produced a low-budget black comedy, *Mortuary Academy*, starring his mentor, Paul Bartel, and produced one of the most acclaimed low-budget films of 1992, the gritty *Guncrazy*, which stars Drew Barrymore as an abused nymphet out on a crime spree. We spoke to him as he was preparing *Fist of the North Star*, a multi-million (that's more than two)-dollar science-fiction film based on the popular Japanese comic book of the same name.

Could you tell us a little about your background, how you got involved in films?

I started a little late in life—I was in my mid-20s. I was running three grocery stores in Idaho, and it seemed like I was living my parents' lives. It was weird—I was doing it to make the money, but I was completely unhappy. I started doing video work in Sun Valley, be it skiers or whatever, realized that film was my passion, and decided to go back to school. I got a divorce, moved to San Francisco, and attended the San Francisco Art Institute, which I chose because of the Kuchar brothers. I absolutely loved it and realized that this is what I had to do.

After I finished up my studies at the Art Institute, I'm driving a limousine and I'm working with some local San Francisco filmmakers, helping Mike and George Kuchar on some of their films while feeling that there's more to this and wondering how to make a living at it. So, approaching age thirty, I was in Mexico on a holiday with some friends and I'd just seen *Lust in the Dust*. I thought, I can probably get a job with Paul Bartel.

So I called Bartel on the phone. He said, "When can you be here?" I said, "I'll be there tomorrow night." So I went over to his house and screened a couple of my student films for him. He said, "Well, I'm doing a couple episodes of *Amazing Stories* for Steven Spielberg. Would you care to come and visit for a day?" I said, "Great, of course I would." So I returned to San Francisco, waited a week or two until the show started, and drove back down for what was supposed to be one day.

Obviously, fresh out of school I was impressed with the whole Amblin setup, the amount of money they were pouring into one television episode—it was really a mini-movie. I've since then made movies for half of what Paul spent on one hour. One day turned into two weeks. I did errands for Paul. His friends liked me and said, "Give this guy a job!" Paul offered me whatever minimum wage was, and I said, "Well, how about fifty bucks a day and I pay my own taxes." At times I was very busy and at times I was left to my own devices. But I had access to everyone Paul had access to—he began sharing contacts, taking me on meetings; Paul was just really great.

While working for him, I optioned for a dollar the first film I co-produced, *Mortuary Academy*. We proceeded to raise financing of a million six or seven hundred thousand dollars, got set up in Culver Studios, and, of course, the money wasn't there on time. I spent four months trying to cast this movie with no real money in the bank while sitting in what was one of the last silent-period stages in town. I thought it was pretty great.

While waiting to start *Mortuary Academy*, I started to write what was to become my second film, *Out of the Dark*. Ultimately, *Mortuary Academy* got funded by RCA-Columbia. Then RCA-Columbia financed *Out of the Dark*.

What was the budget on *Out of the Dark*?

It was about one million six hundred thousand, also. This was in the heyday of video. This was the last twelve months of when the video market was going crazy. I made a comfortable living off that show and then the video market collapsed.

Tell us about it.

At this time [1988], everybody in the world was buying video machines. Video stores were being opened up at a rapid-fire pace and they needed product to fill the shelves. A lot of films hadn't been transferred to video yet, and the stores were just trying to fill this void. Well, all of a sudden there was a glut of lower-budget, independent projects on the market. A lot of people who got into the business then are getting out now. A lot of them are leaving town now.

Has the video market dried up for young micro-budget filmmakers?

Yes, even with the advent of what is soon to be a five-hundred channel system in your home. I think, ultimately, we'll have another surge of supply to fill that market, but right now it's a different world than it was five years ago. It's much more cast-oriented now. The cast can now take an unprecedented percentage of an overall budget because they can motivate a film into a "green light" or "go" position. So I re-evaluated what was going on and decided I wanted to make a film for under half a million dollars. The director and I, as producer, wanted to have a lot of control.

We'd been developing a project that ultimately ended up being called *Liquid Dreams,* which was, much to our amazement, accepted at the Cannes Film Festival in 1991. So here's an example of when a little movie does have the chance to break through. We'd been developing this project with a woman named Barbara Javitz over at Prism Entertainment under the title *The Ritual* to be made at a million and a half. That context was no longer a reality. So we made it as *Liquid Dreams* for three hundred and eighty thousand dollars with pretty much a no-star cast, other than some cameos. We had John Doe from the band X; Paul Bartel was in it. It was a really weird, five-minutes-into-the-future script. We'd given the script to Cassian Elwes, who's the step-son of Elliott Kastner and now a packaging agent at William Morris. He called the director and co-writer, Mark Manos, and I into his office. And he said, "Well, how much do you think you can make this for?" We said, "How about three hundred and eighty thousand dollars?" We knew that we had made a big mistake when he said, "Fine, give me two weeks and you've got the money." We walked out of the office saying, "Boy, were we stupid. I think we should have said half a million." So now, all of a sudden, we had the problem of making this film on three hundred and eighty thousand dollars. And we made it within SAG rules, did it on a semi-legitimate level.

Want to share some production problems?

Well, we figured that if we have to shoot this on location, we can't afford the police, the fire marshal, the permits. Everything's going to be a detriment to the project. And at the same time we wanted to function within the legitimate system. So we went over to what was the Technicolor building, Television Center now, over on Cahuenga. There was a huge room upstairs that was like a lab room, and it was empty. It had terrible sound, but a friend of mine's husband who was in the carpet business got us carpet, and we lined the walls with it to baffle the room. Then we got a bunch of flats and just built sets out of flats. We shot eighteen days, and there was hardly a day under sixteen hours, and some were twenty. Sixteen days were on the set. Two days were off on location. One day was the front of the building, during which there was a drive-by shooting right by our set. And the next night we went out with both cameras— two cameras on a truck that we got for about six hundred dollars when the normal rental on that unit for that night would have been fifteen hundred. It was our big money night and the cameras went down because of some kind of power surge. Eventually, we got cameras sent out to us and saved our butts.

We certainly had a love-hate relationship with this film because, at that budget level, what you're making up for in creative freedom, you're lacking in the money necessary to do it to the best of your ability. There are financial sacrifices and you have to be happy with those sacrifices because there is absolutely no going back on this budget level. But you are making your movie.

I'd say that the film played pretty much every film festival in the world. It ultimately was opened theatrically by a company called Northern Arts, a small, upstate New York company, to highly mixed reviews, although the French absolutely loved it. Maybe there was enough pretense that the French found it endearing. Ultimately, it made the investor money, and I created a housekeeping agreement for myself with a company called Overseas Film Group. They co-produced my next film, *Guncrazy*, for which I put up two-thirds of the private equity. Now I'm doing this film adaptation of a Japanese comic book for them for $2.5 million.

I think the value of the low-budget film is the incredible exposure it gives the filmmakers. It has a large degree of integrity because, often at the lower budget, if you're not forced to do an exploitation film, you have a lot of freedom. We were able to work on *Liquid Dreams* with a composer who did absolutely incredible sound design. We really formed some long-term relationships—the costumer has now done three or four projects with me. The director, Mark Manos, was an editor who also went to San Francisco Art Institute. He has been working for Full Moon in Eastern Europe, and is doing a sexual spin-off on *Cat People*.

How do you maintain quality on a shoestring?

There's a certain amount of compromise. There's a certain amount of calling in favors to keep the quality up. If there's an opportunity to get something for free, you and also the production manager have to ask for it. If the camera package normally costs four thousand dollars, you ask to pay one thousand instead of the four thousand. It's about asking because if you don't ask, you don't receive.

You gotta shoot it in 35mm, you have to pay your people something if it's a commercial venture. And, even at best, when the days get long, you lose people. Quality also comes from the creative team you put together. At that budget level, you're trying to take the talent you've got—whether it be an actor, a makeup artist, a composer—and push the boundaries of what they can deliver, which doesn't always make for smooth sailing. But I think that, in the end, all discussion and arguments are forgiven if people are proud of the final product. The human element is really important when you're trying to get a quality film: try to maintain good, non-screaming relationships with all of your creative people because they're the people who put the quality into it. Part of this is selecting the right people, not picking the first person who comes in and will do it for the number. Somewhere out there is a director of photography, a production designer, a what-have-you, who is willing to do the job because they respond to the material. They may do commercials for five hundred dollars a day and do your show for four hundred a week just because they respond to it. I think that a lot of people in a lot of other venues of the entertainment industry, whether it be music videos, etc., are willing and want to do features. There's a huge talent pool of people who may not have a lot of feature experience.

Is it important to have SAG actors, even though they're more expensive?

Just being a member of SAG doesn't make someone a good actor. Basically, anyone can become SAG if a director or producer wants to Taft-Hartley them and put them in. However, I would say that SAG is the real talent pool.

SAG presents a problem on the financial angle because everybody else is literally working for peanuts while SAG actors are making some four hundred dollars per day, plus the benefits, which add another twelve or twelve-and-a-half percent, and then another seventeen percent that goes to the government. There's a huge injustice in what the actor makes as compared to the crew member. If you defer these people, to even exploit the material, you have to pay them off. As a producer, I feel that whether I'm doing a five-hundred-thousand-dollar show or a ten-million-dollar show, I've got to go with SAG actors in Los Angeles. A lot of people make low-budget films with SAG actors and don't work them through SAG, but there are myriad problems that this can cause.

On a film with a budget of less than five hundred thousand dollars, is it worth getting a theatrical release?

I think that's something the filmmakers, the participants, and the investors have to sit around and discuss. Exposure happens on a theatrical level. If a film is theatrically released, even if it's only in a few major markets, you can increase the video sale. Thirty thousand dollars spent promoting a film on a theatrical level could possibly cause a ten-thousand-units increase at the video level. So I think that theatrical release is super important. Now, if you're looking at the bottom line and somebody wants to spend two hundred and fifty thousand dollars on a theatrical release and you're not going to recoup this cost and all your investors need to get back are two hundred and fifty to three hundred thousand, it's a tightrope walk.

I made *Guncrazy* and sold it to video first. I made a deal with Showtime and received two-thirds of the financing back from them. A fellow named Ray Price, who's now heading up local releasing for Overseas Film Group and used to work with IRS, helped me release *Guncrazy*. He had all the theatrical contacts. For instance, we raised twenty thousand dollars, half from Overseas Film Group and half from Academy Home Video. They gave me a limited window to release it after the Showtime première. The film played the Toronto Festival, the Chicago Festival. It screened at Cannes. It has played at festivals around the world. We took it out theatrically ourselves on the twenty thousand dollars plus ten thousand dollars in goods and services given us for poster, prints, etc. We opened it in probably fifteen to twenty cities. We opened in L.A. for a week—that's all I could get the theater for. We turned around and opened it elsewhere with the reviews we received in L.A. It opened at Film Forum in New York and sold out eight weeks, and for part of that eight weeks it played two theaters. Granted, I was sinking all of my money into postage-sized ads and a larger ad in the *Village Voice*. Vincent Canby, the critic, raved about the film.

As for the video impact of that, Blockbuster, for instance, had made a recommendation on *Guncrazy* for zero to one purchases per store. After the reviews they received from us, Blockbuster increased their purchases in most stores up to two to four units. That increased our sales substantially. I would say that *Guncrazy* would have remained undersold—fifteen or twenty thousand units undersold—if we had not done the theatrical and gotten those reviews. And it certainly elevated the director's career, my career, the D.P.'s; everybody got a good spin off the theatrical release of that film.

Given the choice, would you prefer the looser, more creative low-budget film rather than the big-budget epic?

I think that Abel Ferrara has the right idea. He does the films that are grittier, edgier on a limited budget so that he is able to make them in the manner he wants. At the same time, he goes out and makes eight, ten, twelve-million-dollar movies. To make myself happy, I'd like to do a combination of both. I haven't been blessed with a huge budget, but I'm doing my biggest budget now at two and a half million on *Fist of the North Star*. However, this film is just as difficult to pull off as *Liquid Dreams* was for three hundred and eighty thousand dollars. The skills we learned doing *Liquid Dreams* are totally applied toward this larger-budget film. We still have to beg, borrow, and steal to get this two-and-half-million-dollar movie made because we're trying to do so much more. For a hundred thousand dollars, I'm trying to have seven hundred and fifty thousand dollars, worth of effects.

The relationships forged on *Liquid Dreams* were strong—some of those crew members are still with me. The low-budget film's talent pool feeds the producer's needs for the big-budget film, too. Just like Paul Bartel helped me on my feet, if I help these other filmmakers on their feet, they'll help me later down the road.

Do you have to be more of a dealmaker on the micro-budget level than on the higher level?

No, it can be just as hard to raise a half-million dollars as it is to raise ten million. But there are individuals who are not in the film business who would like to put their feet in the water at a lower-budget level. That's how we got *Liquid Dreams* made and that's how I got *Guncrazy* made.

It's tenacity. If it's the most important thing in your life, you just gotta do it. That gives you the tenacity to not take "no" for an answer. There are a lot of people out there who might give you the money. So, if you stick with it, if you pull off the lower-budget films right, you will get the bigger-budget films.

In making *Liquid Dreams*, was their any problem that you thought at the time was insurmountable?

The big secret to low-budget filmmaking is prep time. Prep time is cheap compared to time in front of the camera.

We had around eight weeks of prep time on *Liquid Dreams*. That eight weeks barely gave us the resources we needed. We used short ends, recanned film. We made do. Insurmountable problems? We initially picked the worst lab in town. Our dailies were lousy. They were literally out of focus.

Did you pick the lab because it was cheap?

It was cheap. That's one place you should never cut corners because it makes people point fingers at the wrong people. You wonder if the focus puller is bad when, in fact, it is the lab. This lab, which shall remain nameless, said, "You'll be back. We're the cheapest in town." I said, "The hell I will." And I went to Fotokem, where I always end up. They have quality and personal service at a reasonable price.

Where can't you cut corners?

A good first-camera assistant. Make sure that the person who is pulling focus on that camera can do it right. And your D.P.

If you're trying to make a low-budget film, don't go out there with a completely unrecognizable cast. Try to get some names. The distributors absolutely need somebody in this day and age to hang the project on. They need to say, "So and so is in it." Get an actor who has some recognition. Otherwise your investors won't get their money out of the film.

Liquid Dreams has a slick look. Is that as important as the cast? What makes your video sale?

I think it's a combination. _Liquid Dreams_ had sort of a music-video feel to it. And that worked. We lit the show with kino-flo light, fluorescent light. They were very easy to move with as opposed to HMIs. We were more limited on our options with kino-flos, but it allowed us to move very quickly. It got us the thirty-plus setups we needed per day on that show. You need something that grabs somebody's attention—slickness or grittiness or name recognition—something that makes them want to buy it. Ultimately, all films have to be sold.

How hard was it to get competent people?

Well, it's time consuming to acquire crew at the low-budget level because you may have to interview twenty or thirty people to find the person you want. And then, the person who you want, after he bites into the project, might find that he can't survive financially or that it's more work than he ever envisioned. Finding the right crew member is also finding the right backup for that member. People like grips don't have a lot to gain out of the project except experience. The way you get crew on a low budget is by giving them the next step—a set dresser becomes a production designer, an assistant camera or second-unit camera becomes a D.P., a wardrobe assistant becomes a costume designer. You give people an opportunity and find the people who can rise to the occasion and deliver.

You have an interesting story regarding the star of _Liquid Dreams_, Candice Daly.

Yeah. When we went to Cannes for the Semaine de la Critique Française, Candice went with us. Prince Albert of Monaco saw the film and saw Candice at a disco later. He absolutely fell in love with her. It was weird because in many ways she looks like a young Grace Kelly, his dead mother. We've never heard from Candice since. We've called her for other productions, but she's disappeared.

Do you have any tips or tricks for young filmmakers coming up?

Yeah. Tenacity is the key.

Credits (as Producer)

Mortuary Academy (1987, RCA/Columbia). Director: Michael Schroeder. Cast: Paul Bartel, Mary Woronov, Christopher Atkins, Wolfman Jack, Cesar Romero.

Out of the Dark (1988, CineTel). Director: Michael Schroeder. Cast: Karen Black, Bud Cort, Divine. Co-written by Levitt.

Liquid Dreams (1991, Overseas Filmgroup). Director/Writer: Mark Manos. Cast: Candice Daly, John Doe, Tracey Walter.

Guncrazy (1992, Overseas/Academy). Director: Tamra Davis. Cast: Drew Barrymore, James LeGros.

Fist of the North Star (1995, Overseas). Director: Tony Randall. Cast: Malcolm McDowell.

Interview *with* NICOLE M. LIBRESCO, Production Manager

After a career in architecture and construction, **NICOLE LIBRESCO** came to movies late. "I see some of these kids come in for P.A. jobs," she says, "I could be their mother." While she sees obvious parallels between film production and her experience managing multi-million-dollar building projects, which taught her all about budgets, schedules, contingency plans, and completion bonds, she has not yet acquired all the knowledge she wants about making movies. Her fail-safe method is to "double-check everything, then double-check it again. Be obsessive!" In the two short years since her career change, she has learned the meaning of "no quote" and steadfastly refused to admit how low the budgets at Concorde were. Before breaking into production, she was a reader for Tribeca in New York and still does occasional coverage for Hollywood companies. When we last spoke, she was producing a dramatic short for a friend.

Could you tell us how you got involved in filmmaking?

I was in New York doing construction management of high-rise buildings and I heard that an architect with whom I worked was having a fifty-year retrospective of his work. I thought it would be a shame not to document it, so I got someone to give me some money and I produced a documentary on the architect and segued into features from there.

How did you get your first job in low-budget filmmaking?

In New York, I did product placement and became the Promotions Coordinator—getting food, clothing, set materials for free—for a movie called *My New Gun*. And I did an internship at New York's Women in Film as well, through their mentor program. And I did production management of documentaries and P.A. gigs on documentaries and commercials.

So you did several documentaries as production manager?

Yes.

Why did you move out here when you had this career going in New York?

As you know, there was the studio-union confrontation then and work slowed to zero. It was clear to me that, if I wanted to do film, I had to go to L.A. I'd be interviewing *for* an assistant production manager or production coordinator job one day, then I'd see the person who got that job when I interviewed as a potential P.A. a few days later. I felt that I would never get hired if I was in competition with people with ten years or more of experience.

But out here there are even more people with experience.

Yes, but there are a hundred and thirty-nine films shooting in L.A. to maybe eight shooting in New York.

So you came out here and got a gig?

Yes, my first production job in L.A. was *Dragon Fire* at Roger Corman's Concorde Studios. I was Production Coordinator and then Second-Unit Production Manager on that.

What is the difference between a Production Coordinator and a Production Manager?

I think the distinctions between the titles Production Coordinator and Production Manager break down a bit in low-budget film because the specific scopes of work perhaps meld a bit. People wear many hats in low-budget. That's not true as you go up to larger budgets. When I was at Concorde, I negotiated equipment contracts for lighting, camera, and grip. That would not be the case for higher-budget—the production manager would be the one negotiating the contracts. I hired crew. A production coordinator wouldn't hire crew in a higher-budget picture. Generally, a coordinator sets up and keeps the production office running, does travel arrangements for cast and crew, is responsible for clearances, and generates a lot of production forms and reports. Production management is more concerned with the whole project, in many cases creating the budget. At Concorde, the production manager generally creates the strip board [an organizational tool outlining shooting days] because they're on payroll whereas an A.D. isn't on yet.

Which job do you prefer?

Production manager, of course.

Why? The money?

On low-budget, pay is never the issue. I'd much rather be creating the budget than be told "here's what the budget is." I like to have the responsibility of making decisions.

Did you have any problems working in the exploitation genres Corman tends to work in?

I needed real experience and credits on my résumé, and that's what I had set out to obtain in as many different genres as possible so I could learn as much as possible in the shortest time period.

What were the budgets on these various shows you production coordinated for Corman?

Around a million.

"Around a million"! As in fifty cents is around a dollar? Okay, no comment. So are there any instances of phenomenal cost-savings that you accomplished while working for Corman?

In general, preparing in advance and having a good shooting schedule and having a script that fits the budget. A good A.D., P.M., rehearsing the actors well are the things that make low-budget easier, more attainable. Having prep time is actually the best thing you can do to get the budget down.

Is that the methodology at Concorde?

It is done at Concorde, and that is one of the reasons why Roger's films are successful. He picks scripts that fit the budget range and locations that work within the budget. You do the project with what you have. If you have two lights for the interior scenes, you do the project with two lights.

If you have a set left over from something else . . . ?

You reuse the set, reuse the props, reuse the costumes.

Were a lot of the same crew on these shows?

It varied. Someone starts out as an electrician. He or she does a couple of things and becomes a best boy. That's a typical promotion. But it's not a given that a technician is going to work on show after show.

Where did the crews come from generally?

I think that with anything, people start out and work at a lower-budget range so that they attain credits. They get their chops at Corman or some other place. Then they go on to other things.

How are these pictures cut, on film or on tape?

Right now they are doing some on tape, but they were mostly done on film. Roger owns a number of Moviolas in the suites at Concorde.

Are there several films shooting simultaneously at Concorde?

There is usually one a month in 35mm that is done at the studio and then maybe three that are done overseas per year. Now I think there are six or eight 16mm films being done concurrently per year. It used to be that you'd be prepping one and shooting one at the same time. Now you're actually shooting concurrently.

Did you do second unit for more than one show at a time?

We did the most for the least. So if the director or the editor comes to you and says, "We need this shot on this movie," and there's a way of fitting it in for the same crew who's doing a pick-up for another movie, then yes. You do the same stuff in the same day if it's possible. Why hire two crews? I did second-unit production management on nine or ten shows.

What's the average shooting time on the second units?

They varied so much.

What do you think is the lowest budget from which you can turn out a movie?

I think you make a movie with whatever you have if you have the passion to do it.

Still and all, there are things that are difficult to scrounge. Can you scrounge film, processing, food?

Film, yes. Processing, no. Food, yes. Processing, titles, lab costs, those kinds of things are difficult to scrounge. Difficult just means "challenging." If you want to make the movie, you're going to go make the movie. You're going to do it whatever way you can. If you make seventy phone calls, you're chance of getting someone to say "yes" is higher than if you make ten phone calls. That's the concept.

I think that what I'd like to say about doing things on the cheap and for free is that there is a misunderstanding that people have today. They think that they can exploit people and get people to work for free. If you can just put your energy into getting products and services for free, then you can go to the financiers and get enough money to pay the crew appropriately and not have to do things without paying people. I don't believe in that.

Have you ever worked on a picture where salaries were deferred?

It's been my experience that deferred really means that you're not going to be paid. It's a euphemism for unpaid work.

What was the longest day you ever shot on a low-budget film?

The longest day was twenty-three hours.

Why did it go twenty-three hours?

It was the last day of shooting and there was a lot to get that hadn't been gotten. We had some problems at the studio that week. And the power went out because a transformer was hit by lightning.

Did you ever encounter a problem as a Production Coordinator or Production Manager that you thought you couldn't solve?

I think anything can be solved. It's just how much are you going to spend to do it and at whose expense will it occur? I got the first and only light (I can't say the name of the company) that comes self-contained, mounted on a truck with its own generator and boom arm, for Concorde. We lit up an entire hillside in Malibu. I had to promise to name my first child after the company, which will sound very strange, and I had to recite the company pledge, which was made up on the spot for me. It was a very expensive piece of equipment that I got for a very good price.

Did your construction experience in New York contribute to your career?

Yes, because I know how to put a high-rise building together. I know exactly who to get for every part of the process. There are many similarities between putting up a building and putting together a movie production: budgeting, scheduling, location, getting a crew from one place to another, contract negotiations. I worked on a high-rise for two years as Construction Project Engineer, which involved managing forty trades of construction and eighty million dollars of cost. One of my subcontractors went bankrupt and I had to call in the payment and performance bond. I had to hire the ironworkers onto our payroll and then redistribute the work to accomplish it on time and on budget. There are similar completion bonds in film. I mean, to a tee, every aspect, there are so many similarities. The project manager would be the line producer. The owner would be the executive producer. A script is the structure.

What advice would you have for newcomers coming in through the low- and micro-budget avenue?

See as many movies as possible. Read as many scripts as you can get your hands on. Worship Joe Bob Briggs. Always keep a vision of what you want to do. Go for your goals. Also, I think that you should read books in all different subjects and work in fields other than film. Explore new technologies, take risks, and continually challenge yourself.

Credits

(as Production Manager)

The Soft Kill (1994, Dream Entertainment). Producer: Larry Rattner. Director: Eli Cohen. Cast: Brion James, Corbin Bernsen, Matt McCoy.

(Second Unit Only)

Dragon Fire (1993). Also Production Coordinator. Director: Rick Jacobson. Cast: Dominic LaBanca, Pamela Runo, Roy Boesch, Chuck Moore.

Unborn II (1993). Also Production Coordinator. Director: Rick Jacobson. Cast: Michele Green, Michael MacDonald.

Symphony (1993). Director: David Tausik.

Saturday Night Special (1993). Also Production Coordinator. Director: Dan Golden. Cast: Billy Burnett, Maria Ford, Rick Dean, Mick Fleetwood, Fred Olen Ray.

Revenge of the Red Baron (1993). Also Production Coordinator. Director: Robert Gordon. Cast: Mickey Rooney, Laraine Newman, Tony Maguire.

Human Target (1993). Director: Jeff Yonis. Cast: Don "The Dragon" Wilson, Denise Buff, Steve James.

Fantastic Four (1993). Director: Oley Sassone. Cast: Alex Hyde White.

Caroline at Midnight (1993). Also Production Coordinator. Director: Scott McGinnis. Cast: Mia Sara, Tim Daly, Judd Nelson, Paul LeMat.

Carnosaur (1993). Director: Adam Simon. Cast: Diane Ladd.

(as Associate Producer)

Concealed Woman. Director: Rodman Flender. Cast: Darryl Hainey.

(as Production Coordinator Only)

One Night Stand (1993). Director: Talia Shire. Cast: Ally Sheedy, A. Martinez, Frederic Forrest, Don Novello.

No Dessert Dad . . . (1993). Director: Howard McCain. Cast: Joanna Kerns, Robert Hays.

Interview *with* STEVE NIELSON, Editor

STEVE NIELSON is an editor who has a hard-nosed attitude toward filmmaking on a micro-budget: "No one wants to be working on a low-budget project. You want to be working on a real movie." Although he has grave misgivings about the whole enterprise, he has managed to bring his craft to bear on a number of messy projects, often saving them in the process. His advice on what to shoot and what not to shoot from an editor's point of view is invaluable for micro-budget filmmakers who may become overwhelmed once they are out there in the field and the unforeseen problems start mounting. After all, it has to cut. Not everything can be fixed in the editing room.

Why don't you tell us a little bit about how you got started in film?

Actually, that goes back to elementary school. A kid moved into my neighborhood who became, and still is, one of my best friends. He's been making movies since he was about six, when he made a twelve-episode serial called *Starboy* on one roll of 8mm film. Through him I fell in love with the process of making movies. I already loved movies, but I fell in love with the *process.* We started making films, and we graduated from super heroes to remaking every Hammer [horror-movie studio in England] film that came out. So I thought maybe it would be interesting to get into movies. I wanted to design titles because that was the hot thing back in the '60s. Then I decided, "No, I wanna be a cameraman." So I went to UCLA and discovered that you had to be a director, that was the only thing worth striving for. I thought I would be a cameraman until that comes to pass, and I was a cameraman for a while on some educational films. But I didn't like the process; I didn't like the kind of thinking you had to do as a cameraman.

When I took the editing class at UCLA, we didn't do the *Gunsmoke* episode. (For those who don't know, still to this day practically every editing class gets the dailies to a scene from a *Gunsmoke* episode and has the opportunity of cutting it. It was not an easy scene to cut. There was a lot of potential for disaster.) I got the material for the *Gunsmoke* scene after I got out of school. So I snuck into an editing room at six o'clock at night, and got hypnotized by trying to solve the scene's problems. When I got hungry, I stepped out of the room to get a candy bar or an apple or something and

found that it was daylight. I'd been in there all night; the time had gone so fast. I decided that this was pretty interesting, and I got into editing.

How is editing a low- or micro-budget film different?

Editors are sort of Monday-morning quarterbacks. You look at the dailies and you say, "My God, what were they thinking about?" But I've been out there in the field, and I know that sometimes they weren't thinking about anything. They were thinking about getting the shot off before the sun went down, while the assistant director was furiously keeping someone from the camera-rental company at bay because the check bounced. So a lot of times you get coverage that's problematic.

Lately I've worked on a lot of films that have been two-week shoots. Their budgets have been close to a half a million dollars. And with that budget you can get a picture that looks pretty good—that looks like a real movie. But there are so many compromises that what comes across is "Hey, this is a real movie. It's just bad." Back in the '50s and '60s, a lot of these low-budget films were bad, but they were a hoot. Now a lot of these movies have a gloss to them, but they're so riddled with compromises that they're not good. Even someone like Fred Olen Ray, who has done a million of these pictures and really knows what you can do and what you can't try for, has sort of a gleeful attitude that makes some of the scenes that don't work invite the audience in on the joke. A lot of times we have SAG actors who are pretty good, but they aren't very good in this picture because they don't have time to work out their characters. It's just "go, go, go," and if it doesn't work, we'll fix it in the editing room, maybe. It's kind of surprising that some of these pictures look as good as they do.

What's the budget range of the films you've worked on?

I worked on a picture called *Microwave Massacre* that was budgeted at about eighty thousand dollars and came in under budget. I think the last picture I did, *Smoke on the Water*, was close to two million.

What are the differences between editing a film that costs eighty thousand and one that costs two million?

Every picture is different.

Mainly, an eighty-thousand-dollar picture is just plain bad. It's kind of futile to undertake. I don't think they make these pictures anymore. Although every so often I pick up a *Dramalogue* and see a dozen pictures where everybody has to work deferred—you know there is no budget. I never see them in video stores; I don't know what happens to them.

What happened to *Microwave Massacre*?

It got released on video tape. It was in the stores for years and years and years.

Why do you think that this one was somewhat successful?

I think it had a good title. It promised T&A, horror, comedy, etc.

What's your biggest challenge on a micro-budget? Not enough time?

Pretty much, although the editor doesn't have the same time constraints as the crew. So that's not so much of a problem. It's just that there are so many compromises during the shoot that you end up with coverage that is almost impossible to put together. You have a scene covered in a wide two-shot and a close two-shot. I remember this movie in which a girl is sitting on the edge of her bed, a kid comes in and offers her a joint. They're passing the joint back and forth. The way the scene was covered, they didn't have all the dialogue in both takes. Unfortunately, there was no correlation between where the joint was and the line of dialogue. So you discover tricks. Cut on a head turn so that the joint pops out of one mouth into someone else's hand. I don't think most people see those little mistakes, but if they do, they're amused by them. I don't know, but I think I disguise them pretty well.

Do directors put more pressure on you because they didn't get the coverage they wanted?

It depends on the producer, what his experience is. Some producers have a pretty good understanding of what you can do in the editing room, and they appreciate editors. I think the general audience doesn't understand editing. You can't see it. You can look at a shot. It's up there for a certain duration. You can say the lighting is pretty or it's this or it's that. A cut isn't up on the screen for any duration of time. So it's more difficult to see a signature, to see what goes into it. I'd say that the biggest headaches I have on these low-budget films, regardless of the budget, are these horrible, loose over-the-shoulder shots, which are really two-shots favoring one person, then the other. Even if the continuity is perfect, it's not going to make a very pretty cut—the people are going to swap places on the cut. Actors have to act. They can watch their continuity to a degree, they can put on their hat in the right sentence, but they're not going to be able to both act and remember their hand motions. So you've got these two-shots and there's no correlation between when somebody is looking up or looking down. It really limits what you can do to make the scene have any pace. That's a problem.

The other problem is that there are so many compromises. It's rare when you're done with a picture that it will be half as good as you hoped it would be. And a lot of producers just won't let go. The picture is what it is, and if you keep fiddling with it forever, it starts deteriorating. Some producers or directors get fixated on one problem. They say, "That's pretty good, but what about this problem." I wasn't aware that that was a problem. There were some problems, but that was the most minor, the least-offensive problem. But that minor problem just rankles them so much that they'll do anything to get rid of it. In the process, the scene gets gutted.

Have you worked on any micro-budget films that you think were successful?

I don't think any film I've worked on, except this last documentary called *Liberation* for the Simon Wiesenthal Institute, tried to be artistically successful.

Successful, then, in telling a story?

I don't understand the tastes of anybody but myself. Yeah, people do say, "Yes, that was a pretty good film." Others say, "It was just hideous." I takes me years after the picture is done to look at it objectively and say, "That wasn't so bad."

Have you worked on any films that presented you with fewer problems, that were easier to cut?

Fred Ray's films are pretty easy to cut because he's experienced at what's possible and what's not. In low-budget films you have to pick compositions that are easy to shoot fast, which doesn't mean just masters. Masters are not easy to shoot. But if you get TV coverage, close-ups, a master to get you started in the scene, which you then cut off when the actors blow their lines and pick up again at the end of the scene, sometimes that is successful.

It allows the editor to play around, and it also allows the actors to get their best shot in there.

How much time in the low-budget range are you given to produce a final cut?

It seems that over the years the time is getting less and less. When I started out, ten weeks was pretty standard for a low-budget picture. Now it seems like they want it faster and faster. What it really means is that you have less time to look at all the takes to make sure you're getting the best performance, which is one of the most important parts of editing. But, at a certain point, they've set up the guidelines and there's nothing you can do about it.

Are most of the films that you've worked on direct-to-video releases?

Nowadays, yes. But when I started out, a lot of things went to theaters. Now it's so hard to get a low-budget film booked into a theater. A lot of them have vanity releases in Cerritos or some out-the-way place. You'll see them advertised in a tiny, one-column ad in the *Times*. That way, when they're selling it to video distributors, they can say it had a theatrical release.

Why do you think that the films are going directly to video rather than having theatrical releases, as they did in the past?

You can make more money on video. It's easier to control the rip-off factor. You can expect the exhibitors will rip off a certain amount of money and distribution will rip off a certain amount of money. There are so many techniques the distributors have for not giving the producer money, which is not so true in video. I've heard a number of people say that they make much more money now that films go to video than when they went out to theaters.

Do you cut the film any differently knowing that it is going to video rather than theaters?

No, not really.

Have you ever cut a feature on tape?

No, I don't want to. I don't like the kind of thinking you have to do to cut on tape.

Is that becoming a trend, cutting on tape for video release?

I think the trend now is toward digital. It allows you to cut like film. It's much easier to extend and shorten shots once you have an assembly. It's kind of the best of both worlds. But the problem on a low budget is that digital equipment is so expensive. I think you can cut about forty percent faster on digital than you can on film, but the producers want it sixty or seventy percent faster. So you end up with a different set of editorial compromises, and I wouldn't say it's either better or worse.

A big problem occurs when you get done with the film: exactly what's wrong that's reparable sometimes takes a while to sink in. And a digital system is chewing up a lot of money each week. You've got to get rid of it, send it back. You don't have time to play around with it after the first cut is done.

Is there any time when you think video is an option for shooting a micro-budget film?

I just think the work is so much worse that most video distributors won't touch it if it's shot on video. A lot of distributors don't want to touch it if it's been shot on 16mm, and a high-quality video transfer from 16mm often can look quite good. A lot of the British TV shows we see, like *Brideshead Revisited*, were shot on 16mm and look quite good.

They now have a "film look" video. They put on a 1.85 matte, and they have some sort of modeling effect that softens it up a bit. I was fooled for a while, but it finally struck me that this isn't right, this is video. It wasn't so much the picture as it was the production. I was looking at the angles and the way they were shooting it. I said, "This looks like it was shot on tape." I looked more carefully and I could see that it was.

Editing documentaries and editing dramatic features, is there a big difference?

There is. But if you're kind of adept at one, you'll be okay with the other.

What film that you've edited had the highest budget?

Smoke on the Water, besides the documentary I'm doing now. I think *Smoke on the Water* is coming out as *Viper,* no relationship to the TV show.

What was your experience like working on that?

Fairly different. The shooting ratio was much higher. It was interesting to see a director have the opportunity to try scenes different ways. Most of the time when I get dailies, it doesn't take very long to know what's going to go together. If there's a close-up of an ashtray with somebody flicking a cigarette and the camera pulls back, that's the opening shot of the scene. But the director of *Smoke on the Water* was able to try different things. It gave me a greater opportunity to put things together in different ways.

Have you worked with any directors who actually think as editors?

Not really. It's interesting when you get a first-time director who plans everything out rigorously, the coverage is so tight that there are no handles. If a cut doesn't work, you're really trapped.

Do you prefer a lot of choices or a director who already has it cut in his or her head?

Again, there are no rules. You can pull it off either way. I think it's always best for a director to go into a scene knowing exactly what he wants and exactly how it's going to cut together, unless he's doing a John Cassavetes-type of film. If you are doing a narrative, it's always best to go in having everything planned out, realizing that when you get out there you may have to start improvising and some things may be scuttled. If you have a plan, the chances of it all working are better.

Would you want an experience where the director gave you tons and tons of footage and you could choose?

Look, no one wants to be working on a low-budget picture. You want to be working on a real movie. I don't think of what I want on a low-budget picture; I think about how I'm going to get out.

So you may have to be more creative on a low budget?

Sure. The whole low-budget world is vast. It's not just these minuscule-budgeted pictures where everybody is new, where everybody may have great theoretical ideas but they've got no experience. Something that's a couple million dollars and has a professional crew and everybody knows what they're doing, that can work. But among the real small-budget pictures, there are only a few pictures that have artistic ambitions, where people are basically willing to put in the time and take however long it takes.

Is the editor ever consulted on a low-budget show or are you just hidden away in a room where they throw dailies at you?

I'm mainly hidden away. Generally, I get a cut before there's much input from anyone. I get my first cut, and then the director looks at it and says, "Great" or "What did you do to my masterpiece?"

Do you think it's important for first-timers especially to consult the editor during the shooting?

If they have a question, yes. The problem is that there are so many ways to do a scene right, and there are so many ways to do a scene wrong. Now, I've been out on a set, and they've said, "Will this cut?" They're not shooting in continuity. It's very difficult for me to say. I don't know what their other coverage was. I don't know how this fits into the scheme. You've got to be sitting there looking at everything to know if something is going to work.

What is _Deadly Dancer?_

I started out cutting four or five low-budget films and got into the union as a sound editor. I cut sound effects for cartoons for about four years. About the time that cartoon sound effects started to be cut on tape, it mainly went non-union. And if you can't make a lot of money cutting sound effects for cartoons, there's no reason to do it. So I sort of started over again in editing. The first film I did after that was called *Deadly Dancer,* which was kind of inspired by *Stripped To Kill,* maybe, or *Flashdance.* It's interesting. The strippers don't really strip. They just dance around and get killed one at a time. The lead actor, a model or something who had never done anything, decided after a week and half or so that he was being ripped off. He decided that he needed more money, a lot more money, and since they were close to half way through the shoot, he decided that he was in a position to get what he wanted. He asked for triple his salary and they said, "Forget it."

After nearly half the film was shot, the lead actor left. They were not going to abandon this project, so they hired a lookalike to play the last two-thirds of the film. It's all in silhouette, over the shoulders, and wide shots. And the guy actually does look a lot like the original lead. So they finished the picture, and they got a third actor to redub everybody.

Do you have any advice for young filmmakers coming into the industry through the ranks of the low- or micro-budget film?

I would say, "Don't do it." The real movie world is one world, and the low-budget world is another. Those two worlds are so separate. If you want to be a director, then, yes, start working on low-budget pictures. But I don't think there's any advantage to it for a craftsperson like an editor or a cameraman. I think it's much better to try to get a job as an assistant editor on bigger features. It seems to me that it would be a lot more profitable spending any number of years being an assistant editor on bigger features because you make contacts. Every once in a while, somebody will latch on to a director who will make the jump. That's possible. That may be beginning to happen for me.

Credits (as Editor)

Lost on Paradise Island (1977). Director: George Leskay.

The Crater Lake Monster (1977). Director: William Stromberg. Cast: Richard Cardella, Glenn Roberts.

The Girls Next Door (1978). Director: James Hong.

Microwave Massacre (1979). Director: Wayne Betwick. Cast: Jackie Vernon.

The Day Time Ended (1980). Director: John "Bud" Cardos. Cast: Jim Davis, Dorothy Malone.

Night Train to Terror (1985). Director: John Carr, Jay Scholossberg-Cohen. Cast: Cameron Mitchell, John Phillip Law, Marc Lawrence.

The Eliminators (1986). Director: Peter Manoogian. Cast: Andrew Prine, Denise Crosby.

Hanging Heart (1987). Director: Jimmy Lee.

Deadly Dancer (1987). Director: Kimberly Casey.

Firehead (1990). Director: Peter Yuval. Cast: Brett Porter, Martin Landau, Christopher Plummer.

Inner Sanctum (1991). Director Fred Olen Ray. Cast: Tanya Roberts, Joseph Bottoms, Margaux Hemingway.

Angel Eyes (1992). Director: Gary Graver. Cast: Monique Gabrielle, Erik Estrada.

Little Devils (1992). Director: Fred Olen Ray. Cast: Robert Vaughn, Priscilla Barnes.

Jeffrey Dahmer: A Secret Life (1993). Director: Rick Bowen.

Night Trap (1993). Director: David Pryor. Cast: Lesley-Anne Down.

Inner Sanctum II (1993). Director: Fred Olen Ray. Cast: David Warner, Margaux Hemingway.

Possessed by the Night (1994). Director: Fred Olen Ray. Cast: Shannon Tweed, Sandhal Bergman.

Viper (1994). Producer: Alan Amiel. Director: Tibor Takacs. Cast: Lorenzo Lamas.

Interview *with* MARK PIRRO, "Mr. Pirromount"

MARK PIRRO is the *wunderkind* of micro-budget filmmaking. He is one of the first people to make a feature in Super-8 (*A Polish Vampire in Burbank*) and one of the few to parlay it into a half-a-million-dollar profit. He does almost everything on his films—he acts, writes, directs, produces, edits, often, he tells us, out of necessity because he's the only one who can "go the distance" on these $2,000-to-$300,000 epics. Yes, that is not a typo: *Two Thousand Dollars!* Pirro has a unique sense of humor in his films which combines satire with such juvenile concerns as losing your virginity. His films are clever and well-made if you can get over their often quasi-Mel Brooksian vulgarity. The titles say it all: *Curse of the Queerwolf, Nudist Colony of the Dead, My Mom's a Werewolf,* etc. Pirro has even done a documentary on himself as well as written a book on "Mini-moguling," as he calls it.

Could you start out by telling how you got involved in film?

I got a camera for Christmas when I was thirteen years old. Basically, that got me going. I would get friends together and make these short films. As I got older, I really got seriously into filmmaking. So I moved out to L.A from New York, and I got a job as a tour guide at Universal. Most of the people I met at Universal were striving to be actors, writers, filmmakers, whatever. After about five years of not really doing anything in film, we decided to pull our talents together and just start making films. I got together with most of the tour guides I met, and I put together a short film called *Buns*. It was kind of cool. We showed it at festivals and we got good comments. That's when I decided that we should continue to make these little mini-movies until someway, somehow we got discovered. We did *The Spy Who Did It Better*, which was a forty-five-minute film. And then we did *A Polish Vampire in Burbank,* which was mainly intended to be a showcase. We never intended to make money with it; we never figured it would make money. None of our other films made money.

Polish Vampire was the first feature film that I ever attempted to do. We tried to show that we could make a feature film— you know, a ninety-minute show—using the people and resources we had available to us. I used whatever money I had. If I had twenty-five dollars one day to buy film, we would shoot: if I didn't, we wouldn't. We'd shoot one day and then we wouldn't shoot again for three weeks. It was that way through-out the whole production.

What was your biggest expense on the film?

Film and processing. At the time, it was about four dollars for every two minutes of film, and, I think, processing was like two dollars. The actors didn't get paid, the locations were free, the props were whatever we could accumulate. We really didn't spend much money on anything but raw stock and processing.

How long did it take you to shoot *Polish Vampire*?

About two and a half years. The guy who did all my sound al-ready had his own mini-studio. That really enhanced the picture a lot—that gave it a professional soundtrack. I kind of took him on as my partner for a while, and we did about five films to-gether.

Who is that?

Sergio Bandera. I was already working on *Polish Vampire* when I met him. He had seen my earlier films and said, "You have some cute films here, but your sound really sucks. Let me work on this picture with you, and I'll give you a really hot soundtrack." For the budget we were working with, the sound was really important. And it just so happened that his roommate, Greg Gross, recorded music, so Greg wrote a score, and I've used him in just about every film I've made since then. The score was free. Well, actually, I gave him a percentage, and Serg got a percentage. And, I think, my cameraman got a percentage. But again, since we never expected to make money, we never expected these percentages to pan out. It did, however, and *Polish Vampire* helped these people get further along in their careers. Like Sergio, he ultimately was discovered by other filmmakers. He does a lot of film work for on low-budget to moderate-budget films. He'll still work on my films, but he's priced himself out of the range for most low-budget filming.

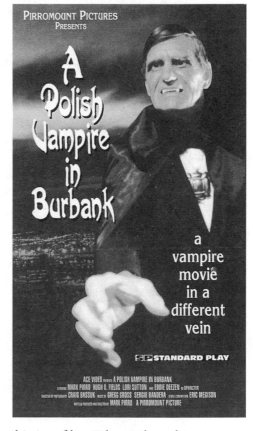

Did you ever get something for free that you never thought you'd get for free?

There were things I thought I'd get for free that I couldn't get for free, like Universal Studios' castle set built for one of their shows, Castle Dracula, which is now used for their the Conan Show. I thought it would be great to use this in a film. When I thought I had permission to use it, when we went to actually use it, it turned out that they didn't want us to use it. We ended up sneaking in there anyway and getting shots. Every time you see the vampire's castle in the film, it was to be that elaborate set, but when they said "no," we just used it for establishing shots. We moved into a friend's garage and built what was to represent one room in the castle. Usually, I write these movies with a very limited budget in mind, and I don't write in anything that I don't think I can get. The problem with Castle Dracula was insurance. The higher-ups didn't want a bunch of kids coming in with cameras and no insurance. So when they said, "No, you can't use it," I was devastated and had to figure out another way. So we went in like tourists with our little cameras strapped to our shoulders, and my friends who were working there kept an eye out to make sure that no authorities showed up.

What was the biggest expense you didn't expect?

It was probably making prints. And it was a useless expense, too. When the movie was done, we made a dupe of it. We showed it in a theater, the Nuart in West L.A., that we rented for an evening—it was like a midnight première. After we showed the film, we decided to make prints of it, which was another big expense that wasn't necessary. When we did *Queerwolf,* for example, we never even bothered to make a final print of the film. What exists is only on video.

You now finish everything on video?

Yes. Why waste the money?

The other thing that caused me problems on *Polish* was the main actor quitting on me after we shot with him for a few months.

Eddie Deezen?

Yes. He didn't want to finish the movie. He just got tired of this guerrilla filmmaking. At first I was thinking, "Well, there goes the film." And then, after thinking about it and rewriting the story, I ended up jumping into the role—taking over as the lead character. Although I cut out a little of the footage that I had shot with him, I managed to save about fifty percent of it. It became the flashback where he is the brother of my character. That set me back a bit. I kept track of every little thing, and if there was any major expense coming up, I would just not do it.

I also did a very low-budget picture called *Nudist Colony of the Dead* for thirty-five thousand dollars.

Also in Super-8?

That was shot on Super-8, 16mm, and 35mm. It was mostly shot in Super-8 because the company that sponsored it, Super-8

Sound, wanted it that way. Then there was a company called Artistic License in Sacramento that put up most of the money. They didn't care what format it was shot in, they just wanted a film they could sell in the various film markets.

When we were shooting Super-8 for *Nudist Colony*, I became frustrated with the medium because it had deteriorated. When I did *Polish Vampire*, there were lots of cameras around, labs, places you could take Super-8 because it was a medium for home-moviemaking. But by the time we did *Nudist Colony*, there was very little competition, so if you didn't like the way the labs processed it, they'd say, "Shoot it in 16. You're lucky we're here." I was really upset with a lot of the footage that was coming back with scratches and splices.

We did Polish Vampire, then we did *Queerwolf*. And in the middle of making *Queerwolf* we were hired by Crown to do *Deathrow Gameshow* in 35mm. When we finished that one, we went back and finished *Queerwolf*.

Time had gone by and I'd written *My Mom's a Werewolf* for Crown. Nothing was happening, so I figured that if Super-8 Sound want me to make *Nudist Colony* for them, and if Super-8 is the only way for them, then I'd do it. About a third of the way through the film, I knew it wasn't working and I told them, "The only way I want to finish this film is if we use some 16mm equipment." They went through the roof because they were promoting their business through this film. So I went to Lloyd's Camera in Hollywood—they've been supporters of mine for years—and they said, "We'll give you a 16mm camera to use. Just bring it back when you're done." So I went back to Super-8 Sound and said, "Look, these guys are going to give me a camera. I'll pay for the film."

I wanted to have some 16mm footage, at least in the crucial scenes. In one scene, we had a helicopter that we got for free, and I knew that if we had a helicopter and the camera screwed up on us, we were sunk. A lot of times I would just make sure that we had the 16mm camera as backup. If the Super-8 looked better, I'd use that. Either way, I wanted to have something good working. Then, of course, it cost more and more money to have the 16mm equipment running at the same time as the Super-8.

It's very rare that a company gives you the supplies and the film to do a feature because a rental company is not in the business of making pictures.

Well, right, but they were in the business of promoting filmmaking in Super-8. There aren't that many filmmakers shooting in that medium. Being the first or one of the first Super-8 feature filmmakers, I had become synonymous with it. I think people got the mistaken opinion that that was the medium I enjoyed working in. Actually, it was the only medium that I could afford! So Super-8 Sound got the idea to sponsor the film, and I was all for it. But when the equipment wasn't delivering, I said, "Hey, this is a film going out there with my name on it that's looking worse than anything I've ever shot. It's not working for me." I took my name and my company name off *Nudist Colony* because I'm really embarrassed by the way it came out. And it could have been the funniest film we made.

We've never seen it, unfortunately, or should we say, fortunately.

And you probably never will. I know Super-8 Sound sells it through *Film Threat* magazine, and I think that's fine. I plan to remake it some day. I retained all the rights to the story. I'm using the original version as a kind of blueprint. If anyone is interested, I show them parts of the film saying, "This is what we shot for a few thousand dollars. I think this could be a really funny film."

Now that Super-8 is virtually dead as a medium, what are the options for someone coming in on a micro-budget?

Well, the cost of Super-8 now, if you try to use the equipment, is almost equivalent to recanned, old, or short-end 16mm film. I think 16 is a good way to go. Also, filmmakers are shooting on video and putting it through a "film look." I've seen some of it, and I'm pretty impressed. It looked better than I thought it would. So there's an option.

If you can make deals, though, you can find companies that will help you out. People are really kind sometimes. Filmmakers must find somebody to sponsor their projects. Maybe they can find a camera shop or a lab. You can get all kinds of deals if you work for them.

Is that your main emphasis in micro-budget filmmaking, making deals?

Oh, sure. I couldn't go out today and make *A Polish Vampire* because most of the people I've utilized over the years have gone on to bigger and better things. And I guess everything is relative when you say "bigger and better things." The things that we used to do with these younger filmmakers—we would make deals with each other and say, "Let's go out and do this and shoot tonight or next week and blah, blah, blah . . ." After you do it a few times, you say, "No, I don't want to do another of these cheap little things. I don't want to stay up till nine the next morning after an all-night shoot." It's hard to get people who are full of that spark. If I ever have to do another film at the level of *A Polish Vampire*, I'd have to find a whole new gang of people because it's really hard to keep that high level of enthusiasm up for more than one or two pictures.

When you are out there finding your team, you have to find fresh people. If you start with twenty people, you're gonna wind up with about three. That's always been the case. Any film I do, if it's low-budget or a low-paying kind of gig, I find that the enthusiasm wears off after a while. On the first day, everybody's all full of excitement. On the second day, it probably cuts by a one fourth, the third day maybe cuts by another fourth. *Polish Vampire* started out with about twenty people, and then there were days when no more than two or three people were on the set. There were times when I was operating the camera *and* in the scene. I'd turn the thing on and run around it. Low-budget filmmaking, at least on this level, is not really fun.

On every one of my films, I would have rather worked with a larger budget. The problem in working at this low level is that you get pigeon-holed. People think that's all you can do because that's all you've done. So, if you do these schlocky little projects, it's hard to break into the two- or three- or five-million-dollar range because you're like a kid—a kid who plays with toys—and you're saying, "I wanna drive a car now."

How do you maintain the semblance of quality in your films with no money?

Of the ten thousand dollars for *Queerwolf,* for instance, four thousand went for buying equipment because Sergio, my sound man, needed certain time-code video equipment so that we could do it a lot easier than we did *Polish Vampire.* We had no synching on *Polish Vampire.* It was, "Let's find a spot where we can start the projector, let's find a spot where we can start the recorder, and hope it stays in synch." *Queerwolf* had synch. Other than that, the locations were free, the actors were free, the lights were cheap—Builder's Emporium clamp-on lights with gels over them. We really didn't have any sets. Everything was shot in houses, apartments, on the street. We had a makeup man who worked at Universal and did the makeup for nothing. So, in reality, there wasn't a lot you could spend money on, other than film and processing.

Some of the filmmakers we've interviewed have said that today you really need actors with a name to sell a low-budget film.

That's very true. There are certain elements that today's movie has to have in order to get exploited. You need names and you need whatever is hot at the moment, which usually means action/adventure. Action/adventure is easy to sell, it seems, because any country understands a car crash or a head blowing up. Kickboxing is also, for some reason, very popular now. I can't tell you how many times I've been approached by people to do a kickboxing film. I suppose that one day I'll wind up doing a kickboxing film, but I have no interest in it whatsoever.

If you don't put a name in it—not even a big name—you'll, at best, get dumped on cable at two in the morning. If you watch Showtime at two or three in the morning, you'll see these graveyards of films that have nothing really going for them.

Is that why you connected with Eddie Deezen?

Yes, although I didn't know at the time that you needed names. Back then, you really didn't. It was ten years ago when we marketed that film, and they were a lot looser in what they would take. Video was still kind of new. They would pretty much say, "Let's put this on and see how it goes." I wanted to use Deezen because I thought that any time you could use somebody who's recognizable, it would give your film credibility. I wasn't thinking in terms of selling it, I was thinking in terms of people looking at the film and saying, "Oh, I know that guy." It makes people feel it's up there with a regular film. I try to stick someone of some worth in every film, even if it's somebody only cultists know. Like I used Conrad Brooks from the old Ed Wood entourage in a couple of my films. Forrest J. Ackerman has been in a couple of my films. That's about the caliber of people I can get.

Do you believe the axiom that in order to get video sales, you have to have some sort of theatrical release?

That's what happened in the case of *Deathrow Gameshow*. *Deathrow Gameshow* had a limited theatrical release—forty cities. That was part of the video deal. Crown signed a deal with Media Home Video, the company that released the film on video, that said that the movie had to play in forty cities for at least a week. That's basically advertisement for the video. You probably don't realize how many times you see a video in a video store on the shelf and you say, "I was meaning to see that film," because you heard about it when it played theatrically. Having a movie playing in major cities and advertised in the newspapers is going to increase your video-rental sales. Some video companies require that.

Did any of your other films have a theatrical release?

My Mom's a Werewolf had a limited theatrical release. *Buford's Beach Bunnies*, a film I did for hire and was disappointed in afterwards, may have gone theatrical in other countries.

That was for Axis?

Yes. I haven't been tracking it, so I don't know what it's done. It pops up on cable all the time, and I believe that August Entertainment, which does Axis's foreign releases, makes theatrical deals with their films.

At one point in your documentary, you claim that *Polish Vampire* made half a million dollars?

Yes.

Was that made in video release?

All of it.

Did you see any of that money or did it all go to the distributors?

Conservatively, I saw about a fifth of it. First of all, Scimitar [the video releasing company] advanced forty thousand dollars against any royalties, which is something they don't do anymore. Very few video-release companies will give advances because so many films don't go anywhere and they lose money. That was probably the biggest deal I've made up front at any time. Then more money was trickling in. It would go through two different middle men and then come to me. I made a deal with a company called Media Gallery who made a deal with a company called Vistar who made a deal with company called Scimitar to release the film. Scimitar pays Vistar, Vistar pays Media, Media pays me, and then I pay the people I worked with on the film. I own eighty percent of *Polish Vampire.* I get checks here and there, checks I don't expect. I didn't know it made as much as it did until I started reading about it in the Scimitar reports. There is even an article in an issue of *Variety* talking about their films, and, at the time, *Polish* had sold eleven-thousand units. They were selling them at something like fifty-nine dollars a unit when they first came out. I just struck a new deal on *Polish Vampire.* They're doing a re-release. They've redesigned the box. They did a really good job of making it look like a whole new film.

What do you think accounts for the success of that film over your other ones?

The backstory. Now most people know the story behind the film. I don't know how people found out about it. It played on USA Network, which may have picked up a few people.

Didn't it play on the syndicated Elvira show?

Almost. We were making a deal, and it looked like it was going through. Cassandra Peterson [Elvira] saw it, her husband saw it; everyone was happy with the film. Then somebody at KHJ [a local TV station] wanted to screen it for the Polish-American Society to make sure that it wasn't offensive to them. Well, whoever they showed it to took offense. They had a problem with the name. They had a problem with the music. They had a problem with the character. So a producer at KHJ said, "KHJ doesn't really want to make any waves right now. So we're gonna pass on it." That's what really determined me to go find a video distributor for it. At that time, we hadn't done anything with it. Then, after we sold it to USA [cable], we made some foreign sales on it. The neat thing about these sales is that when they expire, you can sell it again. The Scimitar deal expired about two years ago and we made a new deal. Now it retails for nine ninety-five. They got both *Polish Vampire* and *Queerwolf* into Music Plus.

Our new video distributor is going to sell them and we hope Blockbuster will say, "Yeah, we'll get some new copies." *Queerwolf* goes out in July. Hopefully Blockbuster will pick it up. Actually, *Queerwolf* went through three different incarnations. First we tried to release it ourselves. We printed up boxes, badly. We made phone calls, used telemarketing. But that didn't work because we didn't have the reach of a big distributor. A Blockbuster is not going to buy from somebody like me calling them on the phone saying, "You wanna take some copies of this movie?" They deal with distributors. Then we tried a video company that went bankrupt after six or seven months, but before they went bankrupt, they made a deal with Scimitar to pick up their trash. Scimitar saw *Queerwolf* and said, "Oh yeah, we know the filmmaker. We'll take it." But that upset me, so I contacted Scimitar and said, "Look, I want the film back." We went back and forth but, eventually, I got the rights back. We've now released it through a better company and, hopefully, we'll get the real surge.

Queerwolf didn't do anywhere near the business that *Polish*

Vampire did. It came in when the market was harder. And, I suppose, the subject matter is kind of hard to get passed. Unless you watch the film, you don't know what you're getting into. And a title like *Curse of the Queerwolf* might turn off some people. Some guys wanted to change the title at one point, but I fought against that because that's the movie I made.

Once you finished *Queerwolf*, how many companies did you go to before you made your first sale?

We went to a lot of companies—I would get lists of video distributors—and a lot of them said, "Don't bother us." But we'd get a few who would be willing to screen the film.

I have learned a lot over the last few years. When we were trying to push this film, we didn't know what we were doing. We would send out a dub of a dub of a dub. They were looking at this grainy, crappy work. It's important to send out a quality product.

What do you think of video?

Express yourself any way that you can do it—video, whatever. Early on, filmmakers should try to make something to show off their abilities, to get work, to get people to get behind them. If you go into it saying, "I'm gonna make this movie. I'm gonna sell it. I'm gonna make a lot of money," I think that your approach is wrong. I think that you're going to be letting yourself down because it's hard nowadays to sell a film that has a cheaper, inferior quality to it.

A lot of filmmakers have said that if you shoot something for video release on video, people can tell. Even though you may never intend to go theatrical, distributors want a film look.

If you're going to release it on video, yes, I still wouldn't shoot it on home video. If you're trying to showcase your abilities as a filmmaker, I'd say shoot in whatever way you can. I know some people who shoot trailers—they shoot a five-minute version of the film they want to make so that they'll have the scenes mapped out and they know exactly what they want to do.

They'll shoot in 16mm or 35mm. And, once they've got their five-minute demo and a script that they may have written, they showcase them around.

The name of the game is to get out of the low-budget range. Most people want to get out of it if they are in it. A writer can write if he has a typewriter or a computer or a piece of paper and a pencil. An actor can go to film classes or act in off-Equity types of shows. As a filmmaker, you have to make a film. Unless you've got some way of doing it, nobody's going to believe that you're a filmmaker. For years, I told people that I was a filmmaker and I had these five- or ten-minute, little Super-8 films that I had done in Upstate New York when I was a kid. That's cute when you're thirteen or fourteen. But I really had to have something I could put together on a reel.

I would continue doing it on that level if I still had the spunk. We'll see how long it takes until I do it again. If I don't get a bigger project going—we're trying to push *Womanator* and *Side Saddle*—and if years go by and nothing happens, you'll probably see me out in the trenches again, preferably with Lloyd's 16mm camera.

Do you think there's any more artistic freedom at this micro-budget level?

I find that the most freedom I've had was on low-budget films. They're all low-budget films, but I mean the lowest budgets.

For instance, do you think that you could make a film like *Curse of the Queerwolf* at a major studio?

If you got a major studio behind it, they would say, "Let's change the title. Let's do this. Let's do that." It all depends on how much faith they put in you. I worked for a large company, Axis, on *Buford's Beach Bunnies*. They hired me because they had seen *Queerwolf* and *A Polish Vampire* and they liked my sense of humor. But once it got underway, they started telling me what to do. They said, "Well, we gotta change this. And we gotta see more of this and less of that." They looked at the film and they didn't get half the jokes. The film that's out there is about twenty percent the film I meant to make.

Since I firmly believe that if it's your dough, it's your show—if you put up the money, I'm going to make you happy—I did a lot of the cuts and changes. I was still fairly pleased with how it turned out. When they released it on home video, there were another twenty minutes of cuts made that I don't think had anything to do with Axis. I think that the home-video release company did their own cuts. I couldn't even watch the version they did.

Could you control the casting on *Buford's Beach Bunnies?*

Everybody I brought in had to be approved by the executives at Axis. For the most part, I cast who I wanted, but there were a couple of times when I ran into problems with agents.

Is it important in low-budget filmmaking to bring along people you've worked with before?

Yes, because these are people you can depend on—like Sergio Bandera, my sound man, and Brian Smith, who produces or co-produces some of my films. As a matter of fact, Brian Smith has gone on to work a lot for Crown. It was all because we went to them for *Deathrow Gameshow,* and I brought him on as producer on that project. Like Glen Campbell, not the singer but the special-effects man who does all the opticals and titles for my films, and my D.P. Craig Bassuk—if you find a good person, hang on to him and bring him with you wherever you go. You're only as good as the people who surround you.

How do you use leverage to get things for free, or convince people to be involved for less money? What advice would you have on that for new filmmakers?

I guess that different filmmakers have different approaches. I've always, or at least as of late, played very humble. I don't say that these films are going to change anybody's career, or that these films are going to do anything for you except get your name up there somewhere. I will always promise screen credit. I start with that. If that's not enough, I'll plead poverty. For instance, when we did *Nudist Colony of the Dead* we needed a helicopter. One of the people working on the film contacted private pilots, asking, "Can you help us out with a helicopter?" Most of them said, "Get out of here." But finally we found a guy who said, "Pay for the gas and you got it." And it went much the same when we needed a courtroom. We called all the courtrooms until we happened to find one that was closed down. The people who had the property said, "Go ahead. You're welcome." I always deal with people as straight as I can. I tell them the whole situation. I tell the truth.

Credits

(as Producer/Writer/Director)

A Polish Vampire in Burbank (1985, Scimitar). Cast: Eddie Deezen, Mark Pirro, Lori Sutton.

Deathrow Gameshow (1987, Crown). Cast: John McCafferty, Robin Blythe.

Curse of the Queerwolf (1988, Pirromount). Cast: Michael Palazollo, Forrest J. Ackerman, Mark Pirro, Conrad Brooks.

(as Writer/Director)

Nudist Colony of the Dead (1991, Pirromount). Producer: Mark Headley.

Buford's Beach Bunnies (1992, Axis International). Producer: Walter Gernert.

(as Writer only)

My Mom's a Werewolf (1989, Crown). Producer: Brian J. Smith. Director: Michael Fischa. Cast: Susan Blakely, John Saxon.

Interview *with* LARRY RATTNER, Writer/Producer

LARRY RATTNER presents himself as that rare commodity in Hollywood—a producer-writer who has not lost his ideals. He has certainly lived up to his homespun motto: "You should never shoot for mediocrity." In producing and co-writing a mini-classic of aberrant L.A., the micro-budget *Horseplayer*, he started out with a list of what he had. ("My father owned a liquor store," he said, "so we decided to have it take place in a liquor store.") He went on to the $1 million *Genuine Risk*. Both are ambitious films that confound the cliché that low-budget films have to be exploitation pieces to succeed. Rattner started out with the king, Roger Corman, in the not-so-proverbial mail room; and, when we spoke, he had just partnered with two Israeli producers in his own company, Dream Entertainment, and finished their first U.S. production, *The Soft Kill*.

Can you tell us how you got involved in films?

I was a Math and Economics major at UCLA who had no intention of being in the film industry. But one of my roommates started taking some film courses, so I decided to take one with her just for fun. Then I took another class and another class. I decided that I might as well do something I enjoy, that I'd be happy with for the rest of my life, so then I started directing all my classes toward business and film. I was never in the film school, I just took the film-school courses.

When I graduated, I decided to try and make film my career. From my last year of college, I started looking into working for various companies in the film industry. And here I am.

What was your first job in the industry?

My first job was working for Roger Corman in the mail room. At that time it was still New World, and nine months later he

sold New World and started his new company. When New World went to its new owners, I went with it. I worked in its Los Angeles branch for theatrical distribution. After a few years of working there, I started working on finance, investment deals, investors' participation, audits, and things of that nature. And, while I was doing that, I was doing other things on the side. I was working on small videos. I was doing a little bit of writing. I was trying to learn as much as possible about production and producing. When New World discontinued their theatrical division, becoming only a television company, I left to produce *Horseplayer*.

How did you come up with the concept for *Horseplayer*?

Kurt Voss and I, Kurt is the director of the movie, came up with it over coffee. Our goal was to come up with a concept that fit into a very small budget. We were shooting to make a film for about two hundred thousand, so we started coming up with elements that we knew we had. At that time, my father owned a liquor store, so we decided to have it take place in a liquor store. And we decided what the basic structure should be and what the story should be about. The writing was very collaborative. We tried to come up with a good story that would be somewhat artistic, but would have commercial elements, because we figured that was the best way to start our careers. The project was character-driven enough that we could hopefully interest actors with some name value, which would make it even more marketable.

You took the high road and stayed out of exploitation. Do you think most new filmmakers can avoid traveling the exploitation avenue?

Well, the business is very different than it was back then. Back then [1990], it was much easier to get a video release. It's more competitive now. What's happened is that the industry is doing well, but everything is becoming more and more geared to the A-pictures. It's just a different market. If someone says, "Listen, I'm going to make a very commercial picture, but it's good," I think that that may be the best way to go because the cast you have and the quality of the story and its commercial potential is what will determine if your film gets distribution and what kind of an advance it will to get. You have to make up for cast weaknesses with a more commercial kind of story—more action or more eroticism. I don't think it makes sense to say, "Okay, I'm going to have a whole bunch of people killed, and I'll have a commercial movie." That doesn't make it either. What's happened is that all these exploitation movies that are just commercial and have nothing redeeming about them don't get distribution now. I think it's a good idea to do something that is commercial. But commercial doesn't mean that it has to be bad. It can be good.

How did you line up the cast for *Horseplayer*?

Michael Harris, who played the artist, we knew. Vic Tayback was a friend of Kurt's family; we approached him early on. Brad Dourif was just someone we came up with who would be right for the role. We pursued him through his agent. We were able to get Sammi Davis because she had the same agent as Michael Harris. So, in the case of Sammi Davis and Brad Dourif, it was a matter of actually submitting the script, and having the agents, the managers, and the actors respond well to it and decide to be part of it. That's another reason why you shouldn't go with an exploitation film: everything comes down to how good the parts are. The weaker the part, the more money you have to pay. I think now, more than ever, actors realize their value to the marketing of a movie. If you get somebody who contributes to the marketing, the money you are going to have to pay could be very substantial. The only way to make it less substantial is to have parts that the actors really want because it's different than what they've done before or because they just think it's a fantastic story.

We shot *Horseplayer* on Super-16mm, so already we kind of had a strike against us. It really shouldn't matter. It should only matter what the actual quality of the film turns out to be. Many movies, like *Enchanted April,* are shot in Super-16 and many movies that are done in Europe are 16mm blown up. But here, if you say, "I've been doing this film on Super-16mm," there's a little bit of hesitancy, as if they're asking, "Is this going to be a professional production?" Those were things we had to go up against.

Hey, we've talked to people who shot in Super-8. So you chose Super-16mm purely for budgetary reasons?

Budgetary.

Is it that large a savings over shooting in 35mm?

It's only a savings if the film doesn't turn out well because then you don't have to blow it up to 35mm, and you've saved on the blow-up costs. If you are going to blow it up, then the costs are probably about the same, and you're probably better off shooting in 35mm. If you go into a film, you have to assume that it's going to succeed. If you go into it thinking that it is not going to turn out, then you probably shouldn't be doing it. I think it's better now to just start with 35mm right away and assume that you're going to succeed. Now, if you are doing something that you figure is going to go straight to video, and you're really trying to do a good film—get a showpiece for yourself—then shooting in Super-16 may not be bad because you're not going to blow it up anyway. But if you're planning to take it to the film festivals and you're going to blow it, then you're better off with 35mm.

How many days did you shoot on *Horseplayer*?

It ended up being about twenty days.

What was your final budget?

We had some problems in the post-production period when we tried to save money. We made some deals with individuals who promised us things they couldn't deliver. You have to be careful all through the production. While you want to save as much money as possible, there are certain places where you really can't. I mean, you can save money, but you can't expect miracles. It's just going to show. We ended up making the movie for about a quarter of a million dollars.

How do you make a film on that low a budget and maintain the quality that you want? Where can you cut corners and where can't you?

There are certain places where you can't cut corners. You have to buy film, and there are certain hard costs in processing and doing the mix. I think every film should be SAG because, even if you are not going to use name actors, it's important that you use good actors, which is especially important for people who aren't experienced, who've never directed a film, never produced a film. They can surround themselves with people who are experienced.

But there are a lot of places where you can cut corners. It is possible to get equipment for free through programs that certain companies have or through favors. It's possible to get things on a deferment basis where you don't have to pay until after the film makes some money. It's possible to get actors for less than they normally get because they really like the film, although you always have to deal with SAG minimums. If you have a location that a friend owns or that you have free access to, it can be a tremendous savings. The ways to save are enormous.

You can't save when you are on a street—you're supposed to have a fireman or else they'll take away your permits. You mess up something like that and it can be a disaster. They can shut down your production. If you get in trouble with SAG, SAG can shut down your production. These are big headaches. You don't want to try and mix a film for two or three thousand dollars just because somebody offers it to you. There's no logic behind that because you may end up with sound that is totally worthless, that will not work, and then what are you going to do?

Also there are certain members of the crew who are crucial. There are certain key positions. If the D.P. shoots out of focus or doesn't know how to move the camera, that could have a disastrous effect on the film. Same thing with the sound person. Getting someone experienced in sound can save you literally tens of thousands of dollars later in the post-production because, if the sound is good, you won't have to do much ADR. You won't have to pay more in terms of adding music to cover background noises.

I don't think you can make a 35mm film for five or ten thousand dollars. You *can* make a film for a couple hundred thousand dollars that others might spend three or four million making, if it's done smartly, and if you have the right people working with you. If you're doing a really small-budget film, it has to be a collaborative effort because you're asking experienced people to work for much less than they usually make. They're doing it because they like the project, because they like the people working on the project. The smaller the budget, the more collaborative it is.

Speaking of crew, how do you find people for a micro-budget film?

It could be someone you know. It could be someone who needs a credit, someone just out of film school who has done only one or two projects. It could be someone who was, for example, a first camera assistant and wants to be a D.P., or maybe someone who has been a hair stylist but has never done hair for a movie. And, depending on the position, it's a matter of how much experience you need. If you have a first-time director, I think it's real important to get a D.P. who's done something before. On the other hand, if you have a director who has a little more experience, and you have a D.P. who's done music videos and maybe some documentaries, maybe that's something to explore.

I don't think there's ever any problem finding the crew. There are so many people who want to get into this industry. The whole key is finding a crew who really understands what you're trying to do in terms of your budgetary constraints and who are going to do their jobs the way they are supposed to.

There aren't many locations in *Horseplayer*.

There were two apartments that are actually the same building. There was a liquor store. We went to the race track for one day. We went to a river bed, which is exterior. And there was the art gallery. That was it.

That must have been pretty cheap.

Yes. What you really want is to spend at least a day at each location. You don't want to move from one location to another location in the middle of the day because of the time it takes you to wrap, move to the new location, and set up again.

If you shoot in a parking lot, it obviously saves you a lot of money because you don't need the art department, you don't need a set. All you need are props. If you do it on the street, some permits, depending on the city, can be very inexpensive. Now, if you go to a location like a restaurant, it can be expensive because you normally ask the restaurant to close down—you not only have to pay them for the rental but for their lost business. You want to design everything so you're in there for the shortest period of time. For example, you're supposed to be three days at the restaurant—two days inside the restaurant and one day outside in the parking lot. That parking lot does not have to be at that restaurant.

For example, the exterior of the liquor store in *Horseplayer* was actually different from the liquor store in which we filmed the interiors because the liquor store for the interiors was in a residential area, which didn't work for the story. So we just picked another exterior. If you compare the doors of the exterior liquor store to the interior liquor store, they really don't match. But you spend so little time looking at the exterior. You're focusing on the actors, and you don't notice it. No one's ever noticed it.

If you're at a location longer, it means that you're saving on prep. Let's say there's a house, a restaurant, and a club. Now, you need to prep and you need to wrap each of those places, unless you're just going in to shoot the them as is. So if you say, "We can make those *two* locations," it's going to be much easier on your art department. And you can always use locations as is. We didn't have to dress the liquor store.

Another thing to consider about very expensive locations is whether it's better to actually put everything on a set. If you're on a set, you don't have to worry about blocking streets. The dressing rooms may be inside the facilities, so you don't have to rent honey wagons [rooms for actors]. Maybe you can pre-light and move lights more easily. One advantage of Super 16-mm on *Horseplayer* was that the rooms were so small that had we had a 35mm camera and equipment, it would have been hard to move the camera. With a set you can move the walls. There's a lot more flexibility. But if you are on an ultra-small budget, your best bet is to use existing locations and shoot them as is. You can have a much smaller crew and an art department that is just someone who's there to make sure all the props are there.

Did you always have theatrical release in mind for *Horseplayer?*

Yes. When you go into it, you have to say first of all, "What is my goal on this movie?" Is it to do a movie to get the experience and try to make it be very profitable? Or are you saying, "I'm a really talented filmmaker. I want this to be the greatest film possible. I want it to go theatrical. I want it to do for me what *She's Gotta Have It* did for Spike Lee and what *Blood Simple* did for the Coen Bros." I think that you should never shoot for mediocrity. If you're saying, "This film is okay. It's not great. But we'll just do it and have fun," that's a totally wrong attitude. If you're striving for mediocrity at the beginning, you can only go down from there. Whatever you're attempting, whether it's a commercial film or whether you say, "This is my showpiece. I want a brilliant piece of work," you should do the best you can.

My opinion is that you always shoot for the theatrical release, while being realistic with what you have. If you have a kickboxing movie, it's going to be very difficult. I think that to be realistic in today's market, you say for a kickboxing film, "Listen, it's got to be a video release or foreign. Maybe it will have a theatrical release in certain places." That's the situation. If you want to go for the theatrical release, you have to put your utmost effort into it.

What you put your utmost effort into is the casting. You have to get name actors because, unless the film turns out to be truly brilliant and wins a lot of awards in all the festivals, even if the film is very good, the film will not get a theatrical release because the market is so hard out there right now. If you really want a theatrical release, you either get some very, very well-known actors or have whoever was investing in the film say, "Here's some money set aside for theatrical release. At least we'll test it." Of course, another way is to come up with a masterpiece. But I don't think you can count on a masterpiece. You shoot to have your film come out that way, but you can never count on it.

How was the theatrical release on *Horseplayer*?

Okay. If you go with a major distributor, you are talking about significant money. On the other hand, there are ways to do a theatrical where, instead of spending two or three hundred thousand dollars, you can spend fifty thousand with a limited release. What I'm talking about is the creation of artwork, the creation of a trailer. I'm not including the cost of a print because you'd only make a couple of prints anyway. And, really, what you're talking about is taking the film from market to market to market and opening it in the right theaters and hoping for good reviews. For that amount of money, you have to exclude New York, and you may have to exclude Los Angeles. You can go to places like Seattle and San Francisco. There are theaters that specialize in these kinds of movies. There are a lot of calendar theaters like the Nuart in Los Angeles used to be. You don't really have to advertise. They advertise on their calendar. They have a following and people will go no matter what. Get a publicist. That's crucial. Place small ads as listings, making sure that critics get there and that it gets good reviews. If it's an art film and you get bad reviews, you're not going to go very far with it. If people respond to the film and it gets good reviews, hopefully your receipts will cover the costs—if not all of them, at least most of them. Then you go to the next city.

Did the theatrical exposure of your film enhance its value when you made video and cable sales?

I think it did. But, in today's market, if it doesn't have a significant enough release, it doesn't really matter because if you open it in Los Angeles and San Francisco, people in Los Angeles and San Francisco and Los Angeles know about the film, maybe. But you've got the rest of the country that knows nothing about it. And most of the people who are not in the film industry don't pay attention to the art-house movies. What I think people are saying now is that unless you have a million-dollar P&A [prints and advertising] commitment, it really isn't going to help video sales. I don't know if it has to be a million dollars. I think that if you have a good film that gets good reviews and you're able to take it through a large part of the country, it will enhance the video sales. But just because you put it in some cities doesn't mean a video company is going to say, "Okay, I'm going to take it." The way theatrical helps for video is that there are so many ads, there are so many billboards, etc., that the public becomes aware of it. That's the key: you have to create an awareness across the whole country.

Was there any point during the film where you encountered a problem that you thought was insurmountable and then solved it?

There are always going to be major problems. That's a given. One of the things you have to do when going into this is be prepared for great problems. And you have to just relax when these problems arise, and think what's the best thing to do. After the first day of shooting, we found that there were scratches on our negative. With Super-16, they take out the sprockets from one side of the camera so that you have more image, and it's very easy for dirt to get up in there. You must clean the camera again and again and again to make sure that it's perfectly, one-hundred-percent clean. We weren't aware of how careful you have to be. So our dailies were getting scratched. Everything was thrown out, which wasn't the best way to start our first day. Another thing that can really destroy a production is the lead actor dying way into the movie. That really has to be a catastrophe. Basically, you have to say that no matter what happens, you'll come up with a solution.

One of the problems we had with our movie was that there had been a mistake—one of our lead actors had been signed to another movie for the same time he was to be doing our movie. The other production was at fault. We weren't at fault. But it had to be worked out. We were able to postpone shooting. We went on hiatus—we didn't shoot for a short period of time while the actor did the other movie, which was outside the United States, and we finished up when he returned. Everything worked out. You just have to say, "No matter what happens, we'll work it out. If it means that we have to rewrite the script, we'll do it. If we have to change the scene and this actor has to leave, we'll do it." As a filmmaker, how successful you are is determined by how well you adapt to these problems. They will always occur no matter what the budget is. On a low budget, you often have a little more flexibility in dealing with them.

After finishing *Horseplayer*, your next film was *Genuine Risk*?

That was actually set up before *Horseplayer*. We weren't sure when *Genuine Risk* was going to start, so we decided to do *Horseplayer* while we were waiting. There was actually a period when both productions overlapped.

What was the budget?

I'd say just under a million.

So your budget was more than three times what it was for *Horseplayer*?

Yes.

Did you find it a very different experience to be working with three times the money?

It was much different because on *Horseplayer* we had Super-16 and no trucks. Everyone had to drive their own cars. The props had to fit in the cars. Our grip-electric consisted of, I think, one person. A lot of the lighting was just light bulbs. Then, all of a sudden, we had trucks, we had grips, we had gaffers. We had a longer shooting schedule—just over four and a half weeks. It was like making a student film, and then making a real film. In terms of results, both of them are real movies, but the *Genuine Risk* experience was much more like a professional film.

We've talked to other filmmakers about how they got a glossy look or a slick design like *Genuine Risk* has without a lot of money . . .

Our production designer, Elizabeth Scott, did a great job on it. She designed the whole look on a very tight budget.

Part of it was making a script that was fit for that budget. Part of it was that the crew was paid more than they were on *Horseplayer* but not their normal rates. And we were very fortunate in terms of the casting. The actors, too, agreed to work for less than their normal rates. Some of the elements that made *Horseplayer* work made this one work.

Was the distribution pattern different on this film?

Here it was pretty much out of our hands. *Horseplayer*, because we put together the financing, was much more collaborative. Here it was pretty much, "Do the movie, deliver it to us, and we'll see you later."

Were you happy with the handling of the film?

Yes, I think so. I mean, there are certain things you look at and say, "I'd do the artwork a little differently, I'd do a different trailer." But overall they did a good job with it.

Do you think *Horseplayer* did well for a film on a micro-budget?

I was really happy with *Horseplayer*. It was at the Sundance Film Festival, which was our goal. Most people really like the film. I think, overall, especially considering what our budget constraints were, yes. It was my first film as a producer. Kurt Voss, the director, had done other stuff at film school, and he had worked on *Border Radio*. He was a little more experienced, but it was the first time he was the solo director on a feature-length film.

You mentioned that distribution has gotten more difficult since you made *Horseplayer*. How?

It used to be that, ten years ago, anything that went on video would do fifty, sixty, seventy thousand units. At that time, video stores were buying everything. What's happened since then is that the public has become more selective. If they can buy *Terminator II* for the same amount as they can buy a quarter-of-a-million-dollar movie that features actors they've never heard of, chances are they're going to get *Terminator II*. The public, pretty much, is not into foreign films or art films. There has to be a reason for them to get it, or they have to really be into that stuff. If they are into that stuff, that's a very small market. If a video store is going to make an investment, and they're paying the same amount of money, or even if they're paying more, for *Terminator II* because they're getting a discount on the independents, they have to figure how many of these so-called B-movies they can afford to get. If they're going to get every one, they are going to have to acquire twenty or thirty a month while they still have to buy twenty or thirty of the A-movies just to keep up with demand. As the demand has become greater for movies with big casts, regardless of their budgets, there's less to spend for movies they haven't heard of or with smaller casts.

The foreign market also has gone through changes. The foreign market had video that was just as strong as the U.S., and when the U.S. video market started to decline, the foreign market was still strong in video. But during the last three or four years that's declined as well. Cable is improving but not as fast as the decline in video. What's happening is that the video distributors are becoming more selective. Where before they'd take any exploitation film and do very well financially, now the production value has to be good. Basically, everybody is getting more sophisticated. That's the bottom line.

So you think the mega-budget films have pushed low-budget films out of the various markets, including video?

I think it's made it more difficult in the sense that the video store has only so much money to spend on product. The video market used to drive everything for independents. It has just been killed. Five years ago, there were so many video companies—New World, New Century, Vestron, and you had Columbia-TriStar actively financing something like twenty movies a year. Maybe sixty or seventy independent movies a year were being financed by these companies. Now they're gone. Now, instead of having twenty or twenty-five video companies, you have something like twelve or thirteen.

So that means that there's a lot less money to finance independent movies. For most people, that's where the financing comes from. It doesn't come from equity investors but from having a good project that causes some company to say, "Okay, I'll finance half the budget for domestic rights, or I'll finance the whole thing and I'll keep worldwide rights." That's much harder now. There's not as much demand. What the stores do and what the studios do, they do because that's what the public wants. You really can't be mad at the studios. You can't be mad at the video-store owners. To them it doesn't matter. All that matters is that they make money. They're just following the interests of the public. Maybe with time it'll change. If it does, it'll change with the culture, not with what the studios do. I think they have some influence, but I think they're basically followers of what the public wants.

Do you have any advice for young filmmakers coming into the low- or micro-budget field today?

The key to everything is the script. The script will determine everything—the crew, the actors, the advance you get to do the movie. What people have to realize is that there can never be enough rewrites. Sometimes you have to rewrite it five or six times, which actually isn't a lot. You have to be very picky. You have to be your own worst critic. The people you trust, even the people you don't trust, you should listen to with a grain of salt. That's really the key to everything.

Credits

(as Producer/Writer)

Horseplayer (1991). Director: Kurt Voss. Cast: Brad Dourif, Sammi Davis, Michael Harris.

Genuine Risk (1990, IRS Media). Director: Kurt Voss. Cast: Terence Stamp, Peter Berg, Michelle Johnson.

(as Producer only)

The Soft Kill (1994, Dream Entertainment). Director: Eli Cohen. Cast: Michael Harris, Corbin Bernsen.

Interview *with* KATT SHEA, Writer/Director

KATT SHEA is part of the new generation of power-feminist filmmakers. Invading the traditional territory of the "old boys," exploitation and genre pictures, she has turned the concepts of those films upside down. Where earlier feminist directors portrayed women as victims, she refuses to buy into the program and instead gives her "gals" teeth (pardon us, Dr. Freud). From erotic thrillers to teenage killers, her protagonists use sex to take control of the screen with a vengeance. In the midst of sleaze or the supernatural, Shea looks for a human understory, like the club dancer who is suicidal over losing custody of her son and "saved" by a vampire in *Dance of the Damned*.

How did you get started in low-budget films?

I was working as an actress in films, some of them for Roger Corman, and I was writing with my partner, Andy Ruben. Our first job was a script for Crown International. We wrote it—first draft, second draft, final draft—for five thousand dollars.

What film was this?

It was called *Patriot*. And what we wrote was never filmed. The director ended up improvising rather than using the script. He was an action director, and if there was a building he could blow up, he'd blow it up, regardless of whether it was written in the script or not.

Wasn't the original script action-oriented?

It was, but the director would blow up anything he saw. He was just into his own thing. It was really a disappointment—we put a lot into that script. There was some heart in it.

What was the film about?

It was about a Navy SEAL. There was a love story. There was a nuclear threat.

So this unpleasant experience with *Patriot* convinced you that you had to become a director?

Yes, I knew that we really had to do something. And Andy was pushing me into it, saying, "It's ridiculous writing for people who don't get it. So do it. Go do it."

Andy and I made a bet. He told me that mussels were poisonous during certain times of the year and I didn't believe him. And, of course, he was right. Losing the bet, I had to go to a strip club. I was really mortified because it was the worst thing he could make me do—go watch women humiliate themselves. I went to The Body Shop [in West Hollywood] and paced back and forth outside trying to get up my nerve to go in. Finally, Andy said, "All right, you don't have to go in. I'm not going to make you go through with this just because you lost the bet." But I said, "I've got to do it." So I went in and I watched the first act, and it wasn't as horrible as I thought it would be. Then I watched the second act, then the third act, and I really became intrigued because I saw these women struggling to be artists and trying to convey something. They were really trying to express their creativity. And all they had to do it with was stripping. I became very fascinated with it; I wanted to do a movie in that milieu.

Of course, I knew the perfect person for it—Roger Corman. All I have to do is say "stripper," and he'll say, "Oh, yes." So I pitched the idea and he was intrigued. The story required that a guy play a woman stripper for the whole movie. Roger didn't think it was possible. He didn't see how it could be done, with G-strings and everything. So I brought this female impersonator into his office who explained in graphic detail how he could wear a G-string without revealing his manhood. And Roger just got so embarrassed. He turned purple. He said, "Okay, okay, just get out of my office."

What was the budget on *Stripped To Kill*?

It was seven hundred thousand dollars.

How were you able to be creative with those money restrictions?

The shooting schedule was actually longer than any of the other movies I made for Roger because once he found out I could do it for seven hundred thousand dollars in twenty-five or thirty days, he cut the budget in half and the schedule in half. The problems in *Stripped to Kill* had to do with time and special effects; things like that just had to go. And not being experienced at that point, we didn't have the time to film things that would help tell the story.

Did we miss something? We thought it told a story.

That's what people tell me, and it got good reviews. It was shown at the Museum of Modern Art. I don't know, I've lost all perspective on it because I know what I wanted to do and what I ended up with. They were very different things.

So you consider that film more of a learning experience?

Yes.

That allowed you to keep working on a micro-budget level at Concorde?

Sure, because I knew what I was in for, what I could count on, and what I couldn't count on.

How did the next one, *Dance of the Damned,* come about?

Well, after *Stripped To Kill*, Roger was really angry with me. He never wanted to see me again because he decided that I had screwed up, and that was that.

"The king" didn't like the film?

No. He hated it. But then *Stripped To Kill* made a lot of money, and it got good reviews. It did well for Roger. I think it was the second-highest-grossing independent film in Europe. So now he was proud of it. He called me up on a Friday and said, "I've got this set that I want to use. Can you come up with something Monday?" It was a nightclub and a house. So Andy and I came up with *Dance of the Damned,* the story of a vampire who kidnaps a waitress. But, since there was a nightclub, Roger said, "If you make her a stripper, it'll be okay." He'd made so much money on *Stripped To Kill* that he figured he needed a stripper in the film to make money.

That film has a slick, stylish look. What was its budget?

Three hundred and fifty thousand dollars, and we shot it in fifteen days. I was trying to do all these visual things to set the mood and tell the story. Everything was lit was very specifically.

How do you accomplish that with so little time and money?

It was extremely difficult. I don't even know how we accomplished it. I look back on it and say, "The energy that it takes to do something like that is just incredible." You've got to keep a crew together and keep them inspired with fifteen-hour days. The crew was inspired by the artistic elements in it, what I was trying to accomplish.

Did you use the same crews in those Concorde films?

No, I used totally different crews.

So you don't think it's that important to carry over the same people for the sake of loyalty and familiarity?

I do, sometimes. And sometimes I think it's important to change because people just start walking through, and there's no way to get them inspired. They're burned out. That was one good thing about this crew: they weren't burned out. They were inspired. They hadn't worked on a movie where the visual elements—the lighting and the colors used, the design—was so important to the storytelling.

And, of course, we entirely changed Roger's sets. The vampire's house was made really modern with very sharp angles. Roger had this old, haunted house and we turned it into a sort of Frank Lloyd Wright design. We were really trying to communicate something about the vampire with the colors, the shades, the textures.

How did you get the actors?

Through auditions.

So they weren't people whom you'd worked with before?

Not on that film. On *Stripped To Kill* I used real strippers, except for Kay Lenz. I had to go to strip clubs and find them, then work with them. I had them doing vanities in my living room.

How do you manage to get performances out of your micro-budget actors?

Again, it's difficult.

Does it have to do with your own acting background?

Yes, it does. I have a lot of sympathy. I know what actors are going through. I know what they feel when they are in front of the camera. No matter how experienced they are, they still have a deep-seated insecurity. You have to deal with the insecurity that they're dealing with. You have to give them a feeling of security and safety, and then they can take some risks. It's really a team effort. They know that they're not alone, that I'm with them.

You know that Roger Corman has already remade *Dance of the Damned*?

Yes. He's remade *Dance of the Damned* and *Stripped To Kill*. He made the Kay Lenz character a reporter, and he used the script.

Was *Stripped To Kill II* thrown together after the first one's success?

You can't imagine how difficult it was to shoot *Dance of the Damned* in fifteen days. We were shooting in the summer and it was one hundred and fifteen degrees. We were working incredibly long hours. The actors had never been through anything like that in their lives. The day we finished shooting, I was ready to collapse. I should have been hospitalized. And then Roger came down to the set and said, "I want you to start *Stripped To Kill II* on Monday because we're going to tear this set down. I want you to shoot just the nightclub scenes. And everything should take place in the nightclub." So I shot a bunch of nightclub scenes, and we wrote a movie around them.

So you shot the nightclub scenes first in *Stripped To Kill II*?

Yes.

And the scenes with the detective in the alley and at her house were shot later?

I kind of knew there was going to be a stripper and there was going to be a detective in the story. I sort of knew what the intrigue was going to be. I knew who the killer was. So I just shot all these nightclub scenes on those *Dance of the Damned* sets. They were dialogue scenes, too—where she's dancing on the table for the detective, where he hands her money on the stage.

How many days was that shoot?

Fifteen.

Do you ever feel that you're sacrificing quality because you're working at such a fast speed?

No. I don't because I'm so determined, so adamant about getting the best quality. I won't move until I know it's really good. *Stripped To Kill II* is so different, though, because so much of it was by the seat of my pants. I thought it was just a big experiment. I had no script, so I decided to have some fun. It was, in fact, the most fun I've had. If it failed, I really had a good excuse. If the story didn't really make any sense, it didn't matter.

Were there some practical locations on these films?

Yes. We didn't make *Stripped To Kill* at Roger Corman's studio. We didn't use sets at all. We got a closed-down nightclub, and then everything else was shot on location. *Dance of the Damned* was all sets. There were a few exteriors. And *Stripped To Kill II* was mostly sets and some locations.

Isn't it hard to acquire locations with no money?

You have to be really creative. You have to look where other people don't look. You have to have very creative art directors, production designers who are really going to do something with the space.

How do you find production designers?

I interviewed the first production designer I worked with. And then, after that, there was a carpenter on *Dance of the Damned* who I thought had some very creative ideas. She solved a big problem. So I hired her to be the production designer on *Stripped To Kill II*.

You must have had moments on these Concorde shows when you thought some problem was insurmountable, was going to shut you down.

On *Dance of the Damned*, the male star [Cyril O'Reilly] had these violet contact lenses. He was only supposed to wear them for eight hours at a time, but he found them so comfortable that he kept them in for twelve hours and got corneal abrasions. His whole face swelled up. I couldn't shoot him. I had fifteen days to shoot the entire movie and my lead actor was going to be out for a week. And Roger was not going to give me any extra time. It looked very dark. I couldn't hire another actor because we'd already shot a few days, and a few days on that kind of schedule is a huge chunk of your shooting time. So I shot Starr Andreeff's [female star of the film] side of every scene. She was constantly in front of the camera. Then I had to go back and shoot Cyril's side when he was better.

Where did you find her? She's not your typical Concorde actress.

She auditioned. I saw her in the lobby, and I asked her to come in.

How important is prep time for these films?

That's everything. I mean, if the film is going to have any kind of style, any kind of look, you really have to prepare in advance. My preparation is not only with the actors—really talking to them and getting them straight—but with the production designer and the D.P. about the look of the film.

If you had to say who the most important crew members were, would you say the D.P. and the production designer?

Definitely, in terms of giving you the look.

Is there any place in making a low- or micro-budget film where you absolutely cannot cut corners?

I suggest that people get the best focus-puller that they possibly can.

You're actually the second person who's told us that. Why?

You can get brilliant D.P.'s for very little money if they can be inspired by the artistic aspects. For me, that's never been hard. I can get artists because they want to do the kind of work I want to do. But to get a focus-puller who's passionate, that's a little more difficult.

What did you do after those films?

I did *Streets* with Christina Applegate. She was great in it. It was shot in nineteen days.

Slightly larger budget?

Five hundred thousand dollars. It was done mostly on location. My carpenter-turned-production designer was the production designer on it. A lot of preparation went into the look of that film.

How did you come up with the concept for that film?

It was really a design concept. I wanted to start with certain colors and take us to another point. I wanted to go from very pale yellows to red, building up this intensity. And the cop stuff was very cold, so that it was totally different from life on the streets.

So the look was based on mood rather than story?

No, it was story-based. It has to be story-based because your first consideration is storytelling.

Did that film have a theatrical release?

It didn't go straight to video. It had a very limited theatrical release.

Do you think there's any value to a theatrical release for a low- or micro-budget film?

I don't think there is really any advantage in the way that Roger Corman releases a movie. It's so small. No one would know the difference. I'm sure it makes a big difference if you do a small release in the way New Line does a small release.

Was the budget for your next film, *Poison Ivy,* much larger?

Three million dollars.

Did you find a world of difference between three million dollars and the salt mines at Concorde?

Yes. It was not as physically taxing. But, you know, there are always the same problems. Not enough time. You always have to make sacrifices and compromises. I think that sometimes the budget limitations force you to be more creative.

Do you think there is more creative freedom in a low or micro-budget film as opposed to a ten- or twenty-million-dollar picture?

I really don't know because I haven't done one yet. I'll be able to tell you more about that next year.

Are you working on something now?

A couple of things that are all that kind of budget. I don't know what's going to go.

Did you find that the theatrical release of *Poison Ivy* helped you at all?

Yes. Even though it was a small release, it did well. I think that it's per-screen average was a little over five thousand dollars for the first week. Tom Pollock from Universal called me and said, "I saw your movie and I really liked it."

How did you come up with the concept for that film?

Peter Morgan and Melissa Goddard, the producers of the film, had a skeletal idea for a film about a girl who moves into a family and takes it over. I was really intrigued, so we just took that pitch and made it our own story.

Did you want Drew Barrymore?

Yes. I do all the casting.

Did you want more time than on the Concorde films to develop the performances?

I like to take an audience through a character, not just show it.

Do you have an art background? Why are your films so design-oriented?

Yes, my father's an artist. I think style is very important. It's like any piece of art. You have certain elements to work with to convey to the audience what you want to convey. If you're not using all the elements, then you're limiting yourself.

Any advice you might give to people coming into filmmaking at a low- or micro-budget level?

Passion is the most important thing. You have to find something you are passionate about. You can't go into it saying, "This is a commercial idea I can sell." I don't believe anything good ever comes of that. You really have to go in with something you really want to make, and then you have to do the best possible job you can with it. It takes a lot of guts and a lot of determination.

Credits

(as Director/Writer)

Stripped To Kill (1987, Concorde). Producer: Andy Ruben. Cast: Kay Lenz, Greg Evigan.

Dance of the Damned (1989, Concorde). Producer: Andy Ruben. Cast: Starr Andreeff, Cyril O'Reilly.

Stripped To Kill II (1989, Concorde). Producer: Andy Ruben. Cast: Maria Ford.

Streets (1989). Cast: Christina Applegate, David Medenhall.

Poison Ivy (1992). Producers: Melissa Goddard, Peter Morgan. Cast: Drew Barrymore, Tom Skerritt, Sara Gilbert.

(as Writer only)

Patriot (1986). Producer/Director: Frank Harris. Cast: Gregg Henry, Simone Griffeth.

Interview *with* ALAIN SILVER, Producer

ALAIN SILVER has produced five features ranging in budget from under $100,000 to $4.5 million and "a bunch of music videos, commercials, documentaries, and other odds and ends." He has also been a "Supervising Producer," which he describes as "not having to hang around until the emulsion on the answer print has hardened," on several other features. He started as a production manager and assistant director on mainstream motion pictures and network TV. We had heard of him as the co-author of *The Film Director's Team*, a book on production management and assistant directing, which was a little dry for our taste, and editor of a great reference book on *film noir*.

How did you get involved in film?

I finished my graduate work at UCLA film school and found out that I couldn't get a job teaching. I already knew I couldn't make a living writing film books, so I took a test to become an assistant-director trainee.

How did you go from that to making micro-budget pictures?

"Micro"-budget? Is that what you guys call these?

"Micro," "ultra-low," those terms seem to capture the flavor, or the price range.

What is the range?

Less than half a million dollars.

Well, I've only made one of those, thank God, which was the first picture that I produced. Although I prepared a picture with a $325,000 budget called *September Song,* which was written like a stage play with ten or twelve long scenes.

Did that picture get made?

No. The company financing it pulled the plug. They spent $30,000 or $40,000 on pre-production and realized they were not going to have the rest of the cash in time. That was too bad, because it was one of those scripts that could have been done pretty well for that price. It was a series of vignettes about Robert Kennedy and Marilyn Monroe, with Brad Davis as Bobby. It was set entirely in Marilyn's mansion and there were only six characters and we could have easily shot it in fifteen days. I had worked on another "Kennedy" picture with a similar structure called *Prince Jack*, which was even more theatrical, being based on a stage play. It cost less than a million, and we wrapped a day early on an eighteen-day schedule and were well under budget.

The first and cheapest picture that you produced is *Kiss Daddy Goodbye*?

Right. Or *Revenge of the Zombie* or *The Vengeful Dead* or who knows what other name some pirate has put on it.

Maybe we can talk about pirating later. Can we start with how you made it?

Sure. After finishing the training program, I was as an assistant director for several years. I worked on features and movies-of-the-week at most of the major studios, and I did a season and a half of a multi-camera sit-com called *Angie*. But back when I was at UCLA, I made my Project 2 for less than $200, and I was convinced that I could produce a feature combining the best of both worlds. I had done a season on *Police Woman* as a trainee, and I believed that if we could shoot those episodes in seven days, the right feature could be made in ten or twelve.

What was your budget?

If I remember correctly, it was $77,000 cash.

For the finished picture?

Yes, but we didn't have that when we started. We had a little less than $40,000.

Was this your own money?

No, we had investors. But we certainly used our own money before we were through.

This book isn't about raising money, but if you don't mind us asking, how did you raise it?

We had a rudimentary sort of prospectus, you know, the kind with articles about how much money low-budget pictures had made—projections, all that stuff. It was pretty crude by current standards; by that I mean that I've done a lot of budgets and projections for people since.

To raise money on other projects?

No, no. Other producers have hired me to prepare budgets for their projects. Sometimes, when they're trying to raise money, I also do projected returns on investment. I've done budgets for Island, Hemdale, Kings Road, Guber-Peters—didn't you read the book *I* co-wrote, *The Film Director's Team?*

It's mentioned in *Hollywood on $5,000, $10,000, or $25,000 a Day*, but we read a lot of books. We love your *film noir* book, though. We crib from it all the time.

Thanks a lot. On *Kiss Daddy Goodbye,* I knew there were SEC rules about money raising, so we only approached people we knew. The biggest investors, who were old friends of my in-laws, put in $15,000. My father-in-law was an optometrist, so instead of "doctor and dentist" money, we had "optometrist" money. That seemed appropriate somehow. Another of the investors played Daddy, the zombie.

"Daddy," this guy on the video box coming out of the grave, was an investor?

Sure.

How did you come up with the concept, the story?

The circumstances on *Kiss Daddy Goodbye* may be rather unusual. We had been preparing another concept alto-gether. It was a horror story set in a small, high-desert community and the "monster" was a Native American guardian spirit who killed archaeologists, bikers, and a greedy real-estate agent, all of whom were profaning the local burial ground.

We scouted locations out in the Anza-Borrego desert at the suggestion of the Director of Photography, Peter Jensen. It was too hot to shoot out there in the summer, so we thought about taking more time to write the script and starting later in the year. Then the Screen Actors Guild went on

"Daddy said we shouldn't. . .ever again."

PENDRAGON FILM LTD. *presents*
KISS DADDY GOODBYE
was it their turn to raise him?
STARRING FABIAN FORTE, MARILYN BURNS, JON CEDAR
WRITTEN BY ALAIN SILVER & PATRICK REGAN
AND RON ABRAMS & MARY STEWART
PRODUCED BY ALAIN SILVER DIRECTED BY PATRICK REGAN

strike. Suddenly everybody we knew was out of work, and we figured that we'd better not let this opportunity go to waste. So the four of us who wrote the script had a story meeting. I had the basic concept about telekinetic powers, and we a made a list of everything we had or knew we could get.

What was on your list?

I can't remember all the details—that was quite a while ago—but some of the cars, the locations, the motorhome. The boy and girl were the director's kids.

How did you get the other actors?

Fabian was the director's ex-brother-in-law—the kids' uncle. One of the associate producers knew Marvin Miller. I had worked on a feature with Jon Cedar, but I didn't contact him. I think someone else knew him from an acting class.

How about Marilyn Burns from *The Texas Chainsaw Massacre*?

One of the writers knew her. Marilyn told us a lot of horror stories about *Chainsaw* and getting ripped off by distributors. In retrospect, we should have paid more attention to her. You should interview her.

We'd love to. Have you got her number?

Not any more. Anyway, we cast the rest of the people by borrowing an office and putting out a couple of notices, probably one in *Dramalogue*.

Was anybody paid?

No. All of the cast were 100% deferred.

Weren't these SAG members?

Most of them, yes.

We take it from your tone that we should move on to the next question. What about the crew?

We had mostly a union crew. I knew Peter [Jensen] from film school and had always liked the way he shot indoors, against windows to have a lot of daylight fill. He was working as a camera assistant on a series at Columbia when the strike hit. Our gaffer and key grip were also off that show. We got a lot of people from Paramount—the makeup woman, the mixer and boom man, the production coordinator. The wardrobe man was from Universal.

None of these union people were paid?

Everyone was completely deferred. They were all laid off from their shows because of the strike. We did have time cards, we did have an accountant, who had been working as the U.P.M. on *Boomer*, keeping track of what they were owed. Part of the problem was that, because everybody was working 100% deferred, we actually hired too many crew people. One of the bit parts was a woman who worked as the assistant director on "Laverne and Shirley"; and when she arrived on location, she said it looked like a real movie, meaning that we had the people and the equipment she would have expected on a regular production. And that slowed us down a bit. We had planned a second unit all along, but I ended up shooting with the second-unit D.P. almost every day. He worked fast; he was an A.S.C. member.

No union problems?

No. A rep for one of the locals did come by the set at the end of the first week. I knew him from when he was an electrician on a pilot I had done at Paramount earlier that year, and when I told him what we were doing, he just said, "Good luck."

We had problems with Cal Trans over road permits. We shot out past Malibu and in the Agoura hills. A highway patrolman stopped us when I was picking up shots on the first day. He didn't stop us for shooting without a permit, but because we were push-starting one of the motorcycles in a parking lot next to the coast highway.

Most of the work was on a small ranch near Agoura and a house in Encino, and at both those places we were tucked in off the street. We got the Sheriff's office set—a small warehouse in Burbank—through a friend. One side was the Sheriff's office, and the other side was the Los Angeles detective's office. At one point, the first unit was shooting in there, and I had the second unit camera about ten feet away, pointing out a doorway shooting a cop pulling up and arresting one of the bikers. Then that cop changed from his uniform to a suit and became the lawyer who gets the biker out of jail. We used him because he was a union extra and owned a police uniform. I shot the arrest with his back to camera. In fact, we didn't even have a police car. We found a black sedan that belonged to one of the crew, and I had that car pull into the foreground so that all that you saw was its front end. When a guy in uniform came into frame, walking from the car as if he had gotten out of it, you assumed that it was a black-and-white. I used the same principal with the bikers. Two would pull up in a long lens shot and the third would walk from the bike that we assumed was just off-screen but which was broken down miles away and not even there. We shot a lot of second-unit sequences out of the back of the Ford Bronco that was used as the Sheriff's car. That was fairly low-profile, but from time to time a real cop would go by and Vilis, the D.P., would just tilt the camera down and cover it with his straw hat.

Where did you get the cars and equipment?

The principal ones were promotional cars from Ford. We had a Bronco, a Lincoln, and a station wagon. Marilyn's Porsche was my car. The main heavy owned or borrowed the motorbikes. We bought the real-estate promoter's car that we sunk into the lake in homage to *Psycho* for about a hundred dollars. It barely ran. I will always remember steering it while it was being towed by a pickup through Malibu Canyon to get to the lake.

When the strike hit, all the productions shut down and returned their equipment, and a lot of rental companies were not prepared to have all this stuff back at once. They didn't have space to store all of it. The rumor was that Mole Richardson had to rent several warehouses for all the lights that came back. We got a package that included a five-ton truck, a small camera van, whatever grip and electric we wanted from the company's inventory, a generator, a dolly, two cameras with sticks, lenses, etc. Since no one else was renting at the time, we paid a few thousand dollars for the run of the show. We also bought Kodak film at 40% off list. The mixer had his own equipment and walkie talkies, which was a deferred rental. The first unit D.P. had his own [Arriflex] IIC, which was the second-unit camera. We owned a pop-top Volkswagen camper, which became both a mobile production office and catering truck, and a motorhome was loaned at no charge. Everybody else used their own cars or pickup trucks.

What else did you pay for?

Not much, really. My mother-in-the law cooked the lunches, and a production assistant brought them out to location. That cost one or two hundred dollars a day. We did pay for some permits and some location rentals. We bought a few clothes and whatever props and set dressing weren't already in place or couldn't be borrowed. We paid for processing and printing the film. The editor and assistants were deferred salaries, like everyone else. We started out in a garage with rented editing equipment. Then we bought a lot of items, and rented a room over at Hollywood National or Zoetrope, as it was known when Francis Ford Coppola owned it. We were in Raoul Walsh alley just off Akira Kurosawa Boulevard next to the Piazza Nino Rota.

Several other people have mentioned that buying equipment is cheaper in the long run.

I don't know about production equipment, but there's always used editing equipment around.

What do you think is the key to making such low-budget movies?

I think the obvious key is prep time, time to make deals and find cheap locations. As it happens, most of the pictures I've done have not had as much prep time as I would have liked. On *Kiss Daddy Goodbye*, we had to finish before the SAG strike was settled and all of our crew went back to their regular jobs.

When was that strike settled?

Two days before we finished shooting. So, on the following Monday, everybody went back to the show from which they were laid off. The lab scratched some film, so we did some reshoots later, but with a much shorter crew.

You talked about speed before. Was the smaller crew faster or slower?

About the same, but lower profile and with a lot fewer lunches.

Was that your only small-crew experience?

No, I've done cable shows and music videos with very short crews.

But no features?

I've done parts of features that way. I co-produced the U.S. portion of an Italian feature that shot three days in Los Angeles and two days in Nevada. There's an example of very little prep time. Four Italians flew into town with a wad of cash on the Thursday before they wanted to start shooting. Starting on the following Monday, we shot two days with a full crew on the standing set of a prison, and we went out of town with only six or seven people.

How did you manage that?

Well, the other local producer and I were both prepping our own features that were to start about a month later, so we used a lot of the crew that were set to do those shows. I was mostly concerned about the stage days because, although the prison set was already there, we had to build an execution chamber and an observation room over the weekend. While I supervised that, the other producer went to Nevada with the location manager. The stage days went well, but the Italians were most impressed by our acumen as producers because of the breakfast and lunch buffets.

What was the name of this movie? Was it shot in Italian?

It was called *The Sleepless Eye*, which was a bad translation of the Italian title, and it later became *The Hidden Lens*, which was not a lot better. It was multi-lingual, and was also shot in France and Italy. The actors spoke the language of whatever country they happened to be in. I never read the entire script. It opened with a celebrated Italian fashion photographer going to a prison to get permission from a murderer to photograph his imminent execution. The last scene was with the American model/love interest at a house in Malibu. We came back and shot that on Saturday after doing the exteriors at the state prison in Nevada.

So they shot the beginning and the end here and the rest in Europe?

Right.

What was the budget?

I don't know what the budget was for the whole picture. I'd guess around four hundred thousand dollars on a twenty-five-day schedule. The U.S. shooting cost fifty-four thousand dollars to pay the crew, rent a soundstage and equipment, and go on location for two days.

Well that sounds like a micro-budget show. You did a movie called *Prime Suspect*. What was the budget on that picture?

I can only reveal that under oath, which I did before the lawsuits were settled. Let's just say significantly under a million.

Lawsuits?

One of the executive producers sold the foreign rights alone for more than the entire budget. Then the "money" executive producer gave the U.S. rights to Sony because he owed them a picture. This was in 1988, long before Sony bought their own studio, back when they were first starting to distribute movies on tape. Then the foreign-sales company reneged on its deal, which caused the lawsuit. They claimed that we'd fired the original director and rewritten the script to save money. We really did all that because the picture didn't make sense.

Have your fired a lot of directors?

On features, just this one. Of course, we picked the one who was living with the leading lady. She wasn't scheduled to work for several days, but it rained, so we had to call her in the day after the firing.

We can imagine how that went.

It was a long day, but I finally convinced her to work and we got it all. We reshot about three days worth of material and still finished only a day over. The bond company was very happy.

You had a bond on this picture?

It was bank-financed, so we had to have it. It was with the Completion Bond Company.

No longer in business, we believe.

True, but not on account of any of my four pictures with them.

When the executive producer gave *Prime Suspect* to Sony, we were told that they had a minimum running time that was quite long—ninety-two or maybe even ninety-five minutes. We had never anticipated that length. We had cut down, or cut out entirely, a lot of poor scenes that we couldn't reshoot. We were barely over eighty minutes, so we shot twenty or thirty inserts and put them in at twice the length we would have normally. Then we stretched the end credits, and found that we were still six minutes short. So the director and I wrote two new scenes using a character who had been referred to but never seen. The plot was so convoluted that we needed more exposition anyway. Then, with a very short crew—five or six people—and three actors, we shot six minutes' worth of film for eight thousand dollars. Sony got the picture, and a month later I read a piece in the *Los Angeles Times,* quoting the man in New York whom I'd delivered the picture to, about how they had sent one movie back for the execs in Japan to look at, and the execs were appalled to see an insert showing a Panasonic television. That was our picture. We couldn't help but laugh. If we hadn't needed to make the inserts so long, they would never have noticed the brand name.

Going back to *Kiss Daddy Goodbye*, you said that you didn't have all the money when you started it. How did you get it finished?

We had a very rough cut—more of an assembly really—that we showed to a few distributors. A guy named Rocco put us in touch with Edward L. Montoro at Film Ventures International. He'd made a lot of money on B-releases, most recently on a *Jaws* rip-off. (He later disappeared under mysterious circumstances.) He sat through this three-hour assembly and said, "Come back when its finished." So we finished it, cutting it down to ninety-two minutes, and then it just sat on a shelf for over a year.

Sounds like it was long enough for Sony.

This was a little before their time. Finally, a girlfriend of one of the assistant directors got a job working for a New York-based distributor during the American Film Market, and she arranged for us to meet with him. By that time, we had a short trailer and a flier. His catalogue was very large and not too upscale: I remember one poster on his wall was for *Invasion of the Blood Farmers*. He had one small hotel room as his AFM suite, which was packed with buyers. We handed him an 8 x 10 flier, which had the key art that became the video box, and he dropped that on his desk and asked us to talk with him out in the hallway, where it was quieter. While we were out there discussing it, a buyer came out holding the flier, asking if this picture was for sale. He offered thirty thousand dollars for Scandinavia and the U.K. We would get our share—twenty-two thousand dollars—on delivering, so that became our new post-production budget. The composer was a friend who worked deferred, and we recorded the music at a small studio owned by a brother of one of the biker actors. We didn't have time to fine-cut the picture. While the director shot a few inserts, I cut in the sound effects and some wild loops on a moviola in a garage. I did the Foley using a video transfer played back on my living-room television, then we rented a kem room to do the music editing and spot for the mix, which took nine hours. The remaining money was spent on the answer print.

So you made money on the U.S. video and other markets?

Not a penny. Pirates made money. We had an arrangement with a local distributor. He could shop the picture, but had to pay a certain amount before any sale was finalized. The lab access letter he got did not permit new prints to be made from the negative without written authorization.

So how did he sell it without your approval?

There was a trial print with a bad soundtrack, which the lab sold him because it was not a "new" print. He filed a second copyright five months after I had, made a one-inch video, reduced the track noise a little bit, and sold it to another company called Wrightwood, who sold it to man who was syndicating the "Elvira, Mistress of the Dark" programs. We found out about it because of two coincidences: the Elvira director was dating a good friend of my wife's who saw my wife's name in the credits, and Cassandra Peterson, who plays Elvira, used to date Fabian. She called and asked him to be in the wrap-around video segments, and then he called us to say that he'd finally gotten paid something for being in this picture.

That's amazing. What happened then?

Nothing. I bartered services with a lawyer who wrote some threatening letters.

Bartered?

I did a budget for him in exchange. That got Wrightwood, who did not know about the origins of the picture, to agree to pay us instead of the pirates. They made the video sale, got sued by the pirates, and went bankrupt. We got no money, and I had a hard time convincing the bankruptcy trustee, who considered *Kiss Daddy Goodbye* an asset of the secured creditor—Wells Fargo Bank—to return the rights. Of course, the unsecured creditors never got anything. It's the same story with a lot of the foreign sales—companies did not pay, went out of business, or bought a pirated copy. I think it was sold four times to Australia: once by Wrightwood and three times by pirates.

Doesn't this bother you?

Sure. But as the FBI agent who investigated one of these pirates told me, these guys who make profits selling pictures like this are not high-profile, and collecting on a judgment is almost impossible. It's not worth suing over.

We ask everybody this next question: Are you going to make any more micro-budget movies?

You know, I am thinking about it. The last picture I produced cost almost a hundred times what *Kiss Daddy Goodbye* did, and it wasn't a whole lot easier. I've got several scripts that I think are commercial. I've had three offers on one of them.

Why hasn't it been made?

Vestron offered us $250,000. to make it, which grew into a three-picture deal. It was a good deal for them but not for us, so we never came to terms. We had another offer to make it for $400,000 with a financier who looked like a crook, so we passed. With the next company, we went in to sign the contracts they'd drafted, only to have them yanked out from under us because the company had been told that comedies didn't sell overseas. This isn't really a comedy, it's a parody of "spunky girl" movies in the *Slumber Party Massacre* vein.

You mean like *Assault of the Killer Bimbos* or some more recent women-in-lingerie-with-Uzis movies?

Not as silly as those. There's a low-budget producer who's called me up several times over the years to ask if I wanted to sell the script, but I've always told him "no." A couple of years ago, a woman at Cannon called to ask if it was true that I had a script about women in prison that could be shot in Israel for $750,000 and could she read it. If this keeps up long enough, this could become a legendary unmade film. In the meantime, I'm tinkering with a vampire script I did a long time ago.

What is this script about, if you don't mind saying? And what's the budget?

I'm not going to give you the whole plot, but it's taken from two Sheridan Le Fanu stories, so it's heavily atmospheric. I'm changing the locale and mostly removing dialogue. It would be micro-budget.

What would you do differently this time?

Make a better picture.

How would you do that?

Well, first off, I'd spend more cash. Not a lot more, but $150,000 to $200,000. Then I would get a better script—better in the aesthetic sense and with characters who would appeal to actors and a story-line that was tailored to this budget level.

Do you have any advice for new micro-budgeteers who are starting out?

One for all and all for one. Find people who want to work for reasons other than a big salary, make it a group effort, and use what money you have judiciously—to maximum effect.

Credits

(as Producer and Supervising Producer)

Kiss Daddy Goodbye (1982). [Also available as *Revenge of the Zombie* and, according to Silver, as *The Vengeful Dead*, although we haven't seen it under that title.] Director: Patrick Regan. Cast: Fabian Forte, Marilyn Burns, Marvin Miller.

Mortuary Academy (1987, RCA/Columbia). Director: Michael Schroeder. Cast: Paul Bartel, Mary Woronov, Christopher Atkins, Wolfman Jack, Cesar Romero.

Prime Suspect (1988, SVS/Sony). Director: Mark Rutland. Cast: Susan Strasberg, Michael Parks, Billy Drago, Doug McClure.

Night Visitor (1988, MGM-UA). Director: Rupert Hitzig. Cast: Elliott Gould, Allen Garfiled, Michael J. Pollard, Richard Roundtree.

Runaway Dreams (1989, Overseas Filmgroup). Director: Michele Noble.

Street War (1990). Director: Robert Hyatt. Cast: Don Stroud, Paula Trickey.

Hold Me, Thrill Me, Kiss Me (1992, Live). Director: Joel Hershman. Cast: Adrienne Shelley, Max Parish, Sean Young, Timothy Leary, Diane Ladd.

Cyborg 2: Glass Shadow (1993, Vidmark). Director: Michael Schroeder. Cast: Elias Koteas, Jack Palance, Angelina Jolie, Billy Drago.

(as Production Executive)

The Ratings Game (1984, Showtime). Director: Danny DeVito. Cast: Danny DeVito, Rhea Perlman.

Interview *with* JIM WYNORSKI, Producer/Writer/Director

JIM WYNORSKI is the classic journeyman director, trained in the Roger Corman school of filmmaking. He's given a project for "X" amount of dollars and he delivers it for that. Unlike other interviewees in this book, however, he has no artistic pretensions, no films that are "dear to his heart." Every film is a potential joy ride and he's a kid at Magic Mountain. He makes them and then promptly forgets them. His parodies are obvious. The running gag in *Hard to Die,* what we've been calling a women-in-lingerie-with-Uzis movie (try saying that three times quickly), is that no matter how many times you shoot a B-movie heavy, they just don't die. As for advice for up-and-coming filmmakers, he is direct and to the point, "Get out. Stay out. I don't want the competition. Screw them . . . the bastards."

Would you like to tell us how you got involved in film-making?

I started in 1981. I was working in advertising in New York and nothing was happening for me. I was doing commercials and I hated it. You wouldn't get any credit for your work anyway. So I decided to pack it in and try my luck here on the West Coast. I always liked movies by Roger Corman, Herman Cohen, and the Woolner Bros.—all these people who had made science-fiction and action pictures in the 1950s and '60s—so I came out here and met a lot of them. And I finally fell in with Roger Corman's company as an advertising representative, creating campaigns for movies.

I had Roger's ear. So, naturally, I started to write scripts. At one point, there was a set that was up for a picture and I said, "I have film I could shoot on the same set." He loved that idea because he'd done it before, so we took my script and we shot it. Originally it was titled *The Mutant*, but there already was a *Mutant* around at that time, so the title was changed to *Forbidden World*.

Did you learn a lot of low-budget filmmaking techniques from Corman?

Yes, I did. I saw how it was done effectively and intelligently—how to go at it without making the costly mistakes that a lot of people were making. Wherever there was a chance to save money, Roger did. I took all that knowledge to heart. Now I'm practicing the same techniques with my own company, Sunset Pictures.

What's the lowest-budget film you ever made?

The lowest-budget film I ever produced, not directed, was seventy-five thousand dollars.

How do you make a film on that kind of micro-budget?

If I said how I did it, then everyone else could do it. I'm going to let it remain my secret. A lot of people have tried to make movies for that budget and have fallen short in a lot of areas.

There are techniques to use, ways to go about it. I will explain a few things. We don't finish on film because it's for videotape delivery only. We shoot on film and we use decent directors of photography so it looks good. We shoot on 16mm and we transfer our 16mm to Betacam tape for assembly for a one-inch delivery of the picture on NTSC and then make a PAL conversion.

A lot of filmmakers we've talked to have differing opinions on the value of a theatrical release of a picture that has to recoup its money in video and cable.

Well, if you have an extra three million dollars or four million and you've made a five-hundred thousand dollar film, does it pay to use that four million to give a theatrical release? No, it does not. But if you spend ten million and you have some name stars, then you may want to spend two million extra to give it a small theatrical release. Maybe it's going to pay off, maybe not.

What's the largest-budget film you've produced or directed?

Seven million dollars. That was *Return of Swamp Thing*.

Do you have radically different approaches on a seventy-five thousand dollar film and a seven million dollar film?

Well, I've worked on budgets from half a million dollars to seven million, and it's not astronomically different. On the higher budget, there are more perks, more time, more chances to do something interesting, but you can still be interesting and do entertaining films on a low budget. You can make a seven-million-dollar bomb or a hundred-thousand-dollar hit. It all depends on your abilities and the script and the actors.

How important is it to attach name actors to a project?

In my estimation, if you have a dramatic project, names are always good. They never are a detriment to your project. However, if you have a project with an interesting hook, you do not need names to sell it. I mention *Friday the 13th* and *A Nightmare on Elm Street*—those films never had stars but they had hooks. I did a film called *Dinosaur Island*, which had no stars, but it had a hook—girls and dinosaurs. So you have to see what the project is and decide whether it's going to be a star-driven project or gimmick-driven project.

What do you think is your most successful film?

That's interesting. I don't know. There would be a difference of opinion depending on whom you asked. In a lot of cases, I worked for hire and I don't know what the returns have been. In the cases where I've done it myself, I've known what monies I've made. I'd have to say *Not of This Earth* with Traci Lords [the ex-porno star]. That was made for three hundred and twenty-five thousand over a twelve-day period in 1987. She was the only star, and her star was not really heavenly at the moment of that film's conception, but at least she was a recognizable name. Her name propelled the film to a very successful run on home video, theatrically, and also on pay-per-view, which was just starting out at that point. I made quite a lot of money on that picture.

What about a film that's closest to your heart?

I have no picture that's close to my heart. The picture that's closest to my heart is the picture I'm finishing, or the picture I'm about to start. The picture I'm about to start right now is a Western, *Hard Bounty*, with Kelly LeBrock.

Would you mind saying what the budget is?

I would definitely mind. It's under five million.

How do you keep a budget low without sacrificing quality?

That's the secret—the secret to a successful career in this business.

Is it preparation time?

It's a knowledge in your head about how to do a shot. You can be in the shittiest room with the barest walls and the lousiest of actors with a sun gun and still do an entertaining shot. Or you can be an amateur and make it look like a bottom-of-the-barrel porno movie, depending on where you put your camera and what you decide to do with the actors. What I learned from Roger Corman is how to make entertaining shots and put them together for an entertaining film. Hopefully I've done that in a number of cases. There's a rule of thumb on how to make a movie, which I learned from Roger, who has made them cheaper than I have. It's a question of depth, foreground, your script. If you start out with a bad script, I don't care how good you are, you are going to fall on your face. You have to start out with a really solid script, a funny script—something that you know is going to make them laugh hard at least three times or make them cry once or make them say "Wow."

Your strong suit seems to be comedy. Is that what you like directing most?

Yes, I let it come out a lot. I'm there to entertain and not to take things too seriously. I think that's why my films have been rather successful. People see that little touch of wry humor.

Have you ever wanted to do an "art film"?

No.

You like the genres that you're in?

The genres that I'm in are very entertaining. When I say "genres," I mean the action-adventure-comedy-sci-fi-horror-fantasy-Western-carchase-kickboxing kind of movies. It's twelve different genres but it's all lumped into the B-film genre. I don't want to do *Howard's End.* I don't think I'd be good at it. I think I'd start to make fun of it. Yes, of course there's room for *Howard's End,* and I respect people who enjoy those kinds of pictures. I don't, and I don't want to make them; that's not why I'm here. I'm here to make the kinds of movies I liked as a kid. I want to make them until I'm no longer a kid.

What kind of movies did you like as a kid?

Sci-fi, fantasy, horror. *The Beast from 20,000 Fathoms, The Thing, It Conquered the World, The Seventh Voyage of Sinbad, King Kong, Them,* Ray Harryhausen films, Roger Corman films, *Attack of the 50-Foot Woman.*

Do you try to bring to your films that sense of wonder that you had watching these movies as a kid?

If you enjoy making the movie and the people seem to be enjoying themselves in the movie, that's infectious and it comes across the screen to the other side. I get a lot of fan letters from kids and girls and guys and people in prison and doctors and lawyers and people from all walks of life. I get letters all the time, all saying how much they enjoyed this picture or that picture. They'll say, "*Sorority House Massacre II* was my favorite picture of yours." Or they'll say, "*Return of Swamp Thing . . .*" or they'll say, "*Hard to Die . . .*" The entertainment that I've tried to put in has come across to them. That's part of the reason I keep doing this. I'm not doing it just for myself, I'm doing it to entertain people. Obviously that's doing some good, and I like the response I get from people.

Are limited locations important when shooting on a micro-budget? For instance, we've mentioned *Hard to Die*, which was mainly shot in one office building. On the other hand, there's *Transylvania Twist*, which is more elaborate.

You're absolutely right. *Hard to Die* was shot on the sets for a film called *Corporate Affairs*.

For the film before that, *Sorority House Massacre II*, I was sitting around at the Corman studios when they had just finished *Slumber Party Massacre III*. And all the sets were in disarray— all the furniture and set dressing had been taken out—all there were were empty sets, the rug, script pages. It was about to be torn down, and I said, "Let's do a film on these sets. And we've got the sets from *Rock and Roll High School, Part II*, also. There's a great basement and a great attic. Why don't I write something with limited characters to fit those sets?"

I wrote the outline, and two of my friends and I sat down and wrote thirty pages a day for three days. Then I went to Julie Corman, Roger's wife, and said, "Julie, let's make this film. We'll make it while you and Roger are on vacation, and it will only cost about one hundred and fifty thousand. Don't tell Roger."

Julie read the script on the fourth day and said, "This is fine." No other company in the world would do this, but she financed the film, without telling Roger, through her own company on the sets that were about to be torn down. We cast it on the fifth day. We literally shot on those sets for six days over the Memorial Day weekend of 1990. And we went on location for one day after that to do exteriors of a house. The whole film was shot in seven days.

The funny thing is, it did very well on home video and extremely well on cable. And it's been playing constantly for the last two years on the pay services. Some people would say that that's my most successful film because it's on almost every week on cable. Maybe that is my most successful film.

Was that film a sequel?

No, it was satire on all the slasher films I hated. But *Hard to Die* was a sequel to *Sorority House Massacre II*. When Roger saw how successful *Sorority House Massacre II* was on home video, he said, "I want you to take the same script and girls and shoot the sets I have left over from *Corporate Affairs*." So I got a majority of the girls back, and I sort of made it my own *Die Hard*, with the same janitor character who was in *Sorority House Massacre II*. I brought him back and kind of redid the film, but this time I went even more far out. I made the janitor character unstoppable. No matter what they did to him, he was going to keep coming back.

Hard to Die has also been a very big, big film. In fact, the Movie Channel had a double bill of *Sorority House Massacre II* and *Hard to Die*, and I went down to Texas to see Joe Bob Briggs [movie series host]. We did our own little tribute to Orville Ketchum, the janitor in both those pictures. He was a fun character to create. The actor in the film was a SAG actor, and because he couldn't use his name, we put "Orville Ketchum as himself" in the credits.

What about a film like *The Haunting of Morella*? The tone was very much like the original Corman film from the '60s. It had the same look to it.

That was my attempt to do something different. There's not a laugh in that picture. I was just trying to do an old-style, Poe picture with a lot of the vibrant colors and that muted darkness—elements that were part of the series of Poe pictures that Roger Corman did. A lot of people like that picture, but I don't. I think that it was an interesting failure for me.

What do you think is the most difficult film you've made?

You know, I don't have one of those. Maybe *Sins of Desire*.

What about *Transylvania Twist*?

I love that film. That was a film nobody wanted to see end. We were laughing all the time. It was a constant, twenty-day party. People did not want to leave the set at the end of the day. I was sort of poking fun, in a nice way, at a lot of different movies that I liked from the old Hammer films of the fifties to the sci-fi films of Roger Corman to *Hellraiser, Friday the 13th*—I took a loving shot at anything I wanted to take a shot at. We just had a blast. I was able to do a lot of different styles of filmmaking. And we had a great art director named Gary Randell who put together some very elaborate sets on a relatively low budget. There were some extremely nice castle locations.

What was the budget?

If I told you, you would not believe it. Seven hundred thousand dollars.

Do you think that creating a feeling of camaraderie is important on a low-budget film, maybe to make up for the low pay?

You cannot create it. It just has to happen. If the actors and the crew gel and they like what they're doing and they like each other, then you're going to have a fun film. One person can come onto a set and bring the whole thing down. I try not to. I try to create a lively atmosphere.

A lot of other low-budget filmmakers have talked to us about how the video market has dried up since 1988 and 1989. Do you agree?

Yes. It's a tougher market to break into.

What are they looking for now?

Gimmicks or good pictures. They're always looking for good pictures. And you can do a good picture for a hundred thousand or a hundred million dollars.

What do you think of the viability of shooting directly on video?

If you want to make a porno film, go right ahead. If you're shooting on video, you better have humping and pumping because that's the only thing that is going to get you out in the marketplace.

So buyers insist on a film look-even if it's going directly to video?

Absolutely.

Do you think the information network, five-hundred channels, is going to revive low-budget filmmaking?

No, because I have a cable service that has seventy-nine channels with movies on ten of them—just ten of them. The rest are shopping, educational, and weather. How much do you watch that stuff? I haven't watched the weather channel in my life. Five-hundred stations . . . let's see what they put on them. Each station is going to have a smaller part of the market. Each station is going to have less money to spend for product. The big ones will still flourish and the small ones will die.

You've made a number of bigger-budget films with more elaborate effects, etc. Is it harder to get those results on the micro-budget scale?

Yes, but that's what people want to see—spaceships, heads exploding, car chases. They don't want to be told about it, they want to see it. You always have to come up with new and inventive films. That's part of the delivery requirement—something that the audience can enjoy and that you can do on your budget.

Yet, at the same time, you can make a successful film on one location like *Hard to Die*.

Trust me when I tell you that that was not an easy film to make. It was a ten-day or eleven-day shoot with tons of squibs, tons of bullet hits. Every time you shoot a bullet out of one of those machine guns, there goes fifty cents. And with retakes and everything else, your budget is adding up. There's a scene where an animated monster comes out of a box, which I put in there to hold the audience's interest. There are some optical effects, but not very many. What makes it successful is the campy humor and the girls with guns parading around in lingerie, which is every man's fantasy. At least it's mine, and I get to live it out with a bunch of really good-looking girls.

How do you come up with the concepts for your films?

That's the toughest part. *Hard to Die* was something like: "I've got sets, so what do I do with them." That's the concept. We shot it and now it's a cable staple; it's what people want to see. Look at *Bikini Carwash Company*, in which I have a small role. That's a film that was made in 16mm for one hundred and twenty thousand dollars. It plays forever on cable. They made a sequel to it, *Bikini Carwash II*. That's what the public wants.

Can the viewer tell the difference when a film is shot in 16mm?

No. Kodak has these new stocks that are as sensitive as 35mm. And if you do a good telecine of your negative, no one will know the difference between 16 and 35.

Have you ever made a film where you just ran out of money?

No.

You always keep it tightly budgeted?

Yes. I always say, "What is the budget?" One million two hundred thousand, one million eight hundred thousand? That's the budget. I look at the budget sheet; I sign off on it. And I usually come in under budget or within a hundred dollars because that's what I'm given and that's what I'll spend.

Do you tend to use crew members whom you've used before?

I use the same people over and over.

Why?

I can depend on them and they won't let me down. They won't pull stunts. They won't smoke marijuana, at least on the set. If they're child-beaters or bigamists off the set, I don't care. As long as they're on the set doing the work, I love them. I have three D.P.s whom I work with a lot.

What about actors?

I have a stock company. Most of them are not names, but some of them are. I've worked with Howard Hesseman a number of times. A lot of unknowns have become known thanks to fans watching my movies.

Again, it's a matter of trusting people whom you've used before?

Yes, they're not going to call in sick. They're not going to come in late, or not know their lines. I've created female scream queens like Monique Gabrielle. I think it's great for them. They're all nice people.

Do you have any advice for young, low-budget filmmakers who are starting in the business?

Get out. Stay out. I don't want the competition. Screw them. Let them try, the bastards.

Credits

(as Producer/Director/Writer)

The Lost Empire (1985). Cast: Melanie Vincz, Raven De La Croix, Angela Aames.

Chopping Mall (1986). Cast: Paul Bartel, Mary Woronov.

Deathstalker II (1986). Cast: John Terlesky, Monique Gabrielle.

Big Bad Mama II (1987). Cast: Angie Dickinson, Robert Culp.

Not of This Earth (1988). Cast: Traci Lords, Arthur Roberts.

The Return of Swamp Thing (1988). As Director only. Cast: Heather Locklear, Louis Jordan, Sarah Douglas.

Transylvania Twist (1989). As Director only. Cast: Teri Copley, Howard Morris, Robert Vaughn.

The Haunting of Morella (1990). As Director only. Cast: David McCallum, Nicole Eggert.

Sorority House Massacre II (1990). Cast: Robyn Harris, Melissa Moore.

Hard to Die (1991). Cast: Robyn Harris.

976-Evil II (1991). Cast: Brigitte Nielsen, Rene Assa, Patrick O'Bryan.

Munchie (1991). Cast: Loni Anderson, Andrew Stevens.

Sins of Desire (1992). Cast: Tanya Roberts, Jan-Michael Vincent, Delia Sheppard.

Munchie Strikes Back (1993). Cast: Andrew Stevens, Lesley-Anne Down.

Dinosaur Island (1993). As co-director only.

Ghoulies 4 (1993). Director only.

Body Chemistry III: Point of Seduction (1993). As director only. Cast: Andrew Stevens, Morgan Fairchild.

Little Miss Millions (1993). Cast: Howard Hesseman, Steve Landesberg.

(as Writer only)

Forbidden World (1982). Director: Allan Holzman. Cast: Jess Vint, Dawn Dunlap.

Sorceress (1983). Director: Brian Stuart. Cast: Leigh and Lynette Harris.

Screwballs (1984). Director: Rafal Zielinsky. Cast: Peter Keleghan, Linda Speciale.

Think Big (1990). Director: Jon Turteltaub. Cast: Martin Mull, Barbarian Brothers, David Carradine.

Beastmaster II (1991). Director: Sylvio Tabet. Cast: Mark Singer, Wings Hauser.

The Final Embrace (1992). Director: Oley Sassone. Cast: Dick Van Patten, Nancy Valen.

House IV (1992). Director: Lewis Abernathy. Cast: Terri Treas, William Katt.

(as Producer only)

Bio-Hazard II (1993).

Dark Universe (1993).

Afterword

While writing a book may be in some respects like making a movie, working a keyboard is nothing like working a set. Making a micro-budget movie is not only hard work, the stress factors of having no margin for error are the kind that put people in the ground before their time. It's easy for us to pontificate or make sarcastic remarks here. In this book, we're working with Monopoly money. So please don't misunderstand our casual sniping at a few of the aspects of the business that peeve us. We write to share information, make a few bucks (very few), and generally get things off our chests.

If you want to succeed in the micro-budget world, preparedness and patience are the real keys. We've been out there spending real money and watching real people bust their butts to get a movie shot in the very few days that so little money permits.

If you have not made a micro-budget picture and are about to embark on your maiden voyage, believe us when we say that there are no mysteries. Anyone can do it with a little information and a lot of determination. Like almost all of the interviewees in this book, we started out pretty blind. A lot of people helped us while we groped around, trying to figure it all out. So we don't share Jim Wynorski's attitude toward newcomers. (He was just kidding anyway, wasn't he?) The whole purpose for writing both this book and *Hollywood on $5,000, $10,000, or $25,000 a Day* was to offer some reasonably priced guidance to people who love movies and want to get into the game.

Finally, if you don't know an answer, and it's not a question we've anticipated here, don't just guess. Find somebody who knows and ask him or her. And when you get it down cold, share the information with someone else. Hey, if you've got some tip or trick that you think we're not aware of, we're not too proud to beg;, help us out, write us and let us know. Who knows, you might end up gracing the pages of *Micro-Budget II, The Return of Gaines and Rhodes*.